50 Reasons Why Christians Should Be Against Conversion Therapy

By James Hosie

1

From a Christian perspective, the belief that "God loves all His children unconditionally" underscores the inherent wrongness of conversion therapy. This fundamental theological truth is central to understanding God's nature and how Christians are called to treat one another.

God's Unconditional Love

- **Divine Acceptance**: The Bible emphasizes God's unconditional love and acceptance. In John 3:16, it is stated, "For God so loved the world that He gave His one and only Son, that whoever believes in Him shall not perish but have eternal life." This love is extended to all people, regardless of their characteristics or behaviors.

- **Parable of the Prodigal Son**: The parable of the prodigal son (Luke 15:11-32) illustrates God's unconditional love. The father in the parable accepts and rejoices over his son's return without conditions, symbolizing God's open and accepting love for all His children.

The Wrongness of Conversion Therapy

- **Conditional Love Imposed by Humans**: Conversion therapy operates on the premise that being LGBTQ+ is something that needs to be changed or fixed, suggesting that

God's love is conditional on a person's sexual orientation or gender identity. This contradicts the core Christian teaching that God's love is unconditional.

- **Psychological and Emotional Harm**: Conversion therapy often leads to psychological and emotional harm, which is incompatible with the loving care Christians are called to show one another. It disregards the emotional and spiritual well-being of individuals, failing to mirror God's nurturing and compassionate nature.

- **Lack of Biblical Support**: There is no scriptural basis for conversion therapy. The Bible does not advocate for changing one's sexual orientation or gender identity as a condition for receiving God's love. Rather, scripture emphasizes that God's love and grace are given freely.

- **Undermining of God's Creation**: Each individual is created by God with inherent dignity and worth. Efforts to change someone's fundamental nature can be seen as a rejection of God's creative work. Psalm 139:14 celebrates this: "I praise you because I am fearfully and wonderfully made; your works are wonderful, I know that full well."

- **Hindrance to True Faith**: By promoting the idea that one's identity must change to be accepted by God, conversion therapy can drive people away from faith. It instills a belief that they are not loved by God as they are, which can lead to alienation from the church and God.

Reflecting Christ's Love

- **Christ's Ministry of Inclusion**: Jesus' ministry was marked by an inclusive love that reached out to the marginalized and rejected. He showed love and acceptance to those society deemed unworthy. Christians are called to follow this example of unconditional love and acceptance.

- **Commandment to Love One Another**: Jesus commands in John 13:34, "A new command I give you: Love one another. As I have loved you, so you must love one another." This love is to be unconditional, mirroring the love Jesus shows us. Conversion therapy, which often promotes conditional love, fails to live up to this commandment.

- **Grace and Mercy**: Christianity is built on the principles of grace and mercy. Ephesians 2:8-9 reminds us, "For it is by grace you have been saved, through faith—and this is not from yourselves, it is the gift of God—not by works, so that no one can boast." Conversion therapy implies that grace is contingent on changing one's identity, which distorts the message of the gospel.

Conclusion

The belief in God's unconditional love is central to Christian doctrine.

Conversion therapy contradicts this belief by imposing conditions on individuals' worthiness of love and acceptance. As Christians, embracing God's unconditional love means rejecting practices like conversion therapy that harm, exclude, and deny the intrinsic value of every person as created and loved by God. Instead, Christians are called to reflect God's love through acceptance, compassion, and affirmation of each individual's inherent dignity.

2

The psychological and emotional harm caused by conversion therapy is a significant factor in understanding its inherent wrongness from a Christian perspective. The teachings of Christianity emphasize love, compassion, and the well-being of individuals. When a practice like conversion therapy inflicts harm on a person's mental and emotional health, it stands in direct opposition to these core Christian values.

The Psychological and Emotional Harm of Conversion Therapy

- **Trauma and Distress**: Conversion therapy often subjects individuals, particularly LGBTQ+ people, to intense psychological stress. The process typically involves attempting to change a person's sexual orientation or gender identity through various means, including counseling, behavioral modification, and even spiritual interventions. These efforts can lead to severe emotional distress, anxiety, depression, and trauma. Many individuals who undergo conversion therapy report long-lasting psychological scars, including feelings of shame, self-hatred, and worthlessness.

- **Increased Risk of Mental Health Issues**: Numerous studies have shown that those who undergo conversion therapy are at a higher risk of developing mental health issues, such as severe depression, anxiety, and suicidal ideation. This is particularly concerning in light of the Christian commitment to protect and care for the well-being of others. By subjecting individuals to a practice that increases their vulnerability to mental health problems, conversion therapy directly harms the very people it claims to help.

- **Undermining of Self-Worth**: Conversion therapy often communicates to individuals that their natural identity is flawed or sinful. This message can severely damage a person's sense of self-worth and identity. It suggests that who they are is fundamentally unacceptable, which can lead to deep emotional and spiritual wounds. This kind of psychological harm is profoundly at odds with the Christian belief that every person is made in the image of God and is loved unconditionally.

The Wrongness of Inflicting Harm

- **Contrary to the Commandment of Love**: Jesus' central commandment in Christianity is to love one another (John 13:34). Love, in its truest form, seeks the good of the other person. Causing psychological and emotional harm, as conversion therapy often does, violates this commandment. Rather than fostering love, conversion therapy inflicts pain, which is antithetical to the love Christians are called to show.

- **Failure to Reflect Christ's Compassion**: Throughout the Gospels, Jesus is depicted as having deep compassion for those who are suffering. He healed the sick, comforted the grieving, and lifted up those who were downtrodden. Conversion therapy, which often results in deep emotional and psychological wounds, fails to reflect the compassion of Christ. Instead of healing, it frequently leaves individuals in a worse state than before.

- **Neglect of Pastoral Care**: Christian pastoral care is supposed to provide support, comfort, and guidance to individuals in a way that nurtures their spiritual and emotional well-being. Conversion therapy, by contrast, neglects this role by imposing harmful practices that damage a person's mental health. This neglect of true pastoral care is a serious violation of Christian responsibility towards others.

- **Ethical Responsibility to Do No Harm**: Christians are called to "do no harm" (Romans 13:10: "Love does no harm to a neighbor. Therefore love is the fulfillment of the law."). Conversion therapy, with its documented psychological and emotional risks, contradicts this ethical mandate. By inflicting harm, it undermines the very essence of Christian love and care.

The Christian Call to Protect and Affirm

- **Affirming Human Dignity**: Christianity teaches that every person has inherent dignity and worth because they are made in the image of God (Genesis 1:27). Practices like conversion therapy, which undermine an individual's self-worth and lead to psychological harm, are inconsistent with the Christian call to affirm and protect this dignity.

- **Prioritizing Well-Being**: The well-being of individuals should be a priority for Christians. Jesus' ministry was focused on bringing wholeness—spiritually, emotionally, and physically. Conversion therapy, with its record of causing psychological harm, fails to align with this focus on holistic well-being.

- **Healing and Restoration**: The Christian faith emphasizes healing and restoration, both physically and emotionally. Rather than inflicting harm, Christians are called to be agents of God's healing love in the world. Conversion therapy, which often leaves individuals with deep psychological wounds, contradicts this mission of healing.

Conclusion

The psychological and emotional harm caused by conversion therapy highlights its profound wrongness from a Christian perspective. A practice that leads to such suffering and distress cannot be reconciled with the Christian call to love, compassion, and care for the well-being of others. Instead of promoting practices that inflict harm, Christians are called to affirm the dignity of every individual, support their mental and emotional health, and reflect the unconditional love and healing grace of Christ.

3

The belief that "Every person is made in the image of God, deserving respect" is a foundational principle in Christian theology that speaks directly to the inherent dignity and worth of every human being. When considered in relation to the wrongness of conversion therapy, this belief highlights why such practices are fundamentally incompatible with Christian values.

Made in the Image of God

- **Imago Dei**: The concept of Imago Dei, Latin for "image of God," originates in Genesis 1:27, where it is written, "So God created mankind in His own image, in the image of God He created them; male and female He created them." This theological truth asserts that every person reflects God's image, regardless of their characteristics, including sexual orientation and gender identity.

- **Inherent Dignity and Worth**: Being made in the image of God bestows upon each person an inherent dignity and worth that is not contingent on their actions, identity, or societal acceptance. This divine image calls for respect and reverence toward every individual as a unique creation of God.

The Wrongness of Conversion Therapy

- **Violation of Divine Image**: Conversion therapy attempts to alter a fundamental aspect of a person's identity—one that is deeply intertwined with how they were created by God. This practice implicitly suggests that certain aspects of the divine image are flawed or need correction, which contradicts the belief that God's creation is inherently good and valuable.

- **Disrespect for Individual Identity**: By seeking to change someone's sexual orientation or gender identity, conversion therapy disrespects and undermines the personhood of individuals. This lack of respect for who they are as God created them is a denial of the image of God within them. Instead of honoring the diversity of God's creation, conversion therapy treats difference as something to be eradicated rather than respected.

- **Contradiction to Christian Compassion**: The Christian call to love and respect others is rooted in recognizing the image of God in everyone. Conversion therapy, which often leads to shame, self-rejection, and emotional harm, does the opposite. It fails to honor the divine image in others by subjecting them to practices that deny their dignity and worth.

- **Dehumanization and Objectification**: When individuals are subjected to conversion therapy, they are often treated as problems to be fixed rather than people to be loved and respected. This objectification dehumanizes them, reducing their complex identities to something seen as defective. Such dehumanization is a clear violation of the respect owed to each person as a bearer of God's image.

Respect and Affirmation of God's Creation

- **Affirming God's Work**: Every person, as a reflection of God's image, is a testimony to God's creative power. To affirm someone's identity is to affirm God's work in their life. Conversely, attempting to change or "correct" a person's identity through conversion therapy can be seen as a failure to trust in God's design and purpose for that individual.

- **Christian Responsibility to Protect Dignity**: Christians are called to protect and uplift the dignity of others, recognizing the sacredness of every life. Practices like conversion therapy, which undermine and attack a person's identity, fail to protect this dignity. Instead of causing harm, Christians are called to be stewards of God's love, offering acceptance and respect.

- **Reflecting God's Love in Relationships**: Christian relationships are meant to mirror God's love, which is unconditional and affirming of the dignity of every person. Conversion therapy, by contrast, imposes conditions on acceptance and love, which can lead to rejection and alienation. This conditionality is contrary to the unconditional respect that should be afforded to every person made in the image of God.

Conclusion

The belief that every person is made in the image of God and deserving of respect fundamentally opposes the practice of conversion therapy. Such therapy not only disrespects the God-given identity of individuals but also undermines their inherent dignity and worth. As Christians, the call to recognize and honor the image of God in each person requires rejecting practices like conversion therapy, which harm rather than heal, and instead embracing a love that affirms the diverse ways in which God's image is reflected in humanity.

4

The commandment of Jesus to "love our neighbors as ourselves" is one of the most profound and central teachings in Christianity. This commandment, found in Matthew 22:39, "Love your neighbor as yourself," reflects the essence of Christian ethics and morality. When viewed in relation to the wrongness of conversion therapy, this commandment reveals how such practices violate the very core of Christian love and compassion.

The Commandment to Love Our Neighbors

- **Universal Love**: Jesus' command to love our neighbors extends to all people, regardless of their backgrounds, identities, or circumstances. This love is not conditional or selective but is meant to be as inclusive and unconditional as God's love for humanity. It calls Christians to show empathy, understanding, and respect for others, treating them with the same care and consideration they would want for themselves.

- **Empathy and Compassion**: Loving our neighbors as ourselves requires us to put ourselves in others' shoes, to understand their experiences and struggles. It demands a compassionate response to the suffering of others, where we seek to alleviate pain rather than inflict it. This empathetic love is at the heart of Christian living, guiding how we interact with and treat others.

The Wrongness of Conversion Therapy

- **Contradiction of Love**: Conversion therapy, by its nature, contradicts the commandment to love our neighbors. Instead of offering unconditional love and acceptance, it seeks to change or "fix" an individual's sexual orientation or gender identity. This approach is rooted in judgment and rejection rather than love and affirmation. It conveys the message that a person must change to be loved, which is the antithesis of the unconditional love Jesus teaches.

- **Infliction of Harm**: Conversion therapy often inflicts psychological, emotional, and even physical harm on those who undergo it. This harm directly violates the command to love others as ourselves, as it treats people in ways that we would never want to be treated. The practice fails to protect the well-being of individuals and instead subjects them to pain and suffering, which is incompatible with Christian love.

- **Denial of Dignity**: Loving our neighbors as ourselves means recognizing and respecting their inherent dignity as children of God. Conversion therapy, however, denies this dignity by implying that a person's natural identity is flawed or unacceptable. This denial of dignity is a form of rejection and dehumanization, which stands in stark contrast to the respect and honor that Jesus' commandment demands.

- **Failure to Foster True Relationship**: Jesus' commandment is about fostering genuine, loving relationships with others. Conversion therapy, which often results in alienation, shame, and broken relationships, fails to foster the kind of loving, supportive relationships that Jesus advocates. Instead of building community and understanding, it often leads to division and hurt.

The Christian Call to Unconditional Love

- **Embracing Others as They Are**: To love our neighbors as ourselves means to embrace them as they are, without demanding that they conform to our expectations or ideals. Conversion therapy imposes conditions on acceptance, suggesting that love and approval are contingent on changing one's identity. This conditional love is contrary to the unconditional love that Jesus exemplifies and commands.

- **Support and Affirmation**: Loving our neighbors means supporting and affirming them in their journey of life, providing encouragement and care. This includes respecting their identity and the way they experience the world. Conversion therapy, which seeks to change a fundamental aspect of a person's identity, fails to offer this kind of support and affirmation.

- **Protecting the Vulnerable**: Jesus consistently showed concern for the vulnerable and marginalized, those who were often rejected or mistreated by society. Conversion therapy often targets vulnerable individuals, particularly LGBTQ+ youth, who are at risk of significant harm. Loving our neighbors requires protecting these vulnerable individuals from practices that would harm them.

Conclusion

The commandment to love our neighbors as ourselves is a guiding principle that reveals the wrongness of conversion therapy from a Christian perspective. This practice violates the very essence of Christian love by inflicting harm, denying dignity, and imposing conditional acceptance. Instead of reflecting the love and compassion that Jesus commands, conversion therapy fosters rejection, pain, and alienation. As Christians, we are called to reject such practices and instead embody the unconditional, affirming love that Jesus demonstrated, ensuring that every person is treated with the respect, dignity, and compassion they deserve.

5

The claim that "The Bible does not endorse conversion therapy practices" is crucial when considering the wrongness of such practices from a Christian perspective. The absence of biblical support for conversion therapy highlights that these practices are not rooted in the teachings of Scripture but are rather a modern invention that contradicts the spirit of Christian love and compassion.

The Bible and Human Identity

- **Creation in God's Image**: The Bible begins with the affirmation that all people are created in the image of God (Genesis 1:27). This foundational belief underscores the inherent dignity and worth of every person, regardless of their sexual orientation or gender identity. The Bible does not suggest that aspects of this God-given identity need to be changed or "corrected" through practices like conversion therapy.

- **Diversity of God's Creation**: Throughout Scripture, there is an acknowledgment of the diversity of God's creation. The Bible celebrates differences within the human family without prescribing that everyone must conform to a single mold. This understanding contrasts sharply with the aims of conversion therapy, which seeks to erase or alter certain identities rather than embrace them as part of God's diverse creation.

Lack of Biblical Endorsement for Conversion Therapy

- **Absence of Support**: Nowhere in the Bible does it advocate for or even mention conversion therapy—the practice of trying to change a person's sexual orientation or gender identity. The lack of biblical endorsement for such practices suggests that they are not a part of God's design or will for human relationships and identity.

- **Misuse of Scripture**: Some proponents of conversion therapy attempt to use specific Bible verses to justify their practices. However, these interpretations often take passages out of context or misapply them in ways that distort the Bible's overall message of love, grace, and acceptance. For example, passages that discuss sexual ethics in the Bible do not provide a basis for coercive practices aimed at changing a person's identity.

- **Focus on Spiritual Transformation**: The Bible emphasizes spiritual transformation—turning away from sin and growing in Christlikeness. However, this transformation is about the renewal of the heart and mind in Christ (Romans 12:2), not about altering one's fundamental identity, such as sexual orientation or gender identity. The focus is on spiritual growth and moral integrity, not on forcing individuals to conform to human-made norms.

The Wrongness of Conversion Therapy

- **Contradiction of Biblical Principles**: Conversion therapy practices contradict several core biblical principles. First, they undermine the biblical concept of God's creation, implying that certain aspects of who a person is are mistakes to be corrected. Second, they violate the commandment to love others unconditionally, as conversion therapy often inflicts psychological and emotional harm rather than offering love and support.

- **Harmful Outcomes**: The Bible calls for the protection and care of the vulnerable, and it condemns actions that cause harm to others (Proverbs 31:8-9; Matthew 25:40). Conversion therapy, which has been shown to lead to increased rates of depression, anxiety, and suicidal ideation among LGBTQ+ individuals, particularly youth, results in significant harm. These outcomes are clearly incompatible with the biblical mandate to love and protect others.

- **Lack of Fruitful Evidence**: Jesus taught that a good tree is known by its fruit (Matthew 7:17-20). The "fruit" of conversion therapy—broken relationships, mental health struggles, and alienation from the church—indicates that it is not a practice that produces good, life-giving results. Instead, it often leads to spiritual and emotional damage, which is evidence of its fundamental wrongness.

The Call to True Biblical Compassion

- **Acceptance and Love**: The Bible repeatedly calls Christians to love one another (John 13:34-35) and to bear each other's burdens (Galatians 6:2). True biblical compassion does not seek to change someone's inherent identity but rather seeks to support, affirm, and walk alongside them in love. This means accepting people as they are, rather than imposing harmful practices in the name of conformity.

- **Focus on Healing, Not Harm**: Jesus' ministry was marked by healing, restoration, and the affirmation of individuals' dignity (Matthew 11:28; Luke 4:18). Conversion therapy, which has been linked to significant emotional and psychological harm, stands in stark contrast to the healing ministry of Jesus. The Bible calls Christians to be agents of God's healing, not to participate in practices that cause harm.

Conclusion

The Bible does not endorse conversion therapy practices, and attempting to use Scripture to justify such practices misrepresents the true message of the Bible. Conversion therapy not only lacks biblical support but also contradicts key Christian principles of love, compassion, and the affirmation of human dignity. As followers of Christ, Christians are called to reject practices that cause harm and instead embrace an approach that honors the image of God in every person, offering love, acceptance, and support rather than coercion and condemnation.

6

The misuse of biblical texts to justify harm is not only inappropriate but also deeply contrary to the core teachings of Christianity. This principle is particularly relevant when considering the practice of conversion therapy, which some have attempted to justify using Scripture. However, such justifications are a distortion of the Bible's true message and an affront to the Christian call to love, compassion, and the protection of human dignity.

Misuse of Biblical Texts

- **Selective Interpretation**: Some proponents of conversion therapy selectively interpret certain Bible verses to argue that being LGBTQ+ is sinful or that it is necessary to change one's sexual orientation or gender identity to be in accordance with God's will. However, these interpretations often ignore the broader context of Scripture, which emphasizes love, grace, and the inherent worth of every person as created by God.

- **Ignoring the Fullness of Scripture**: The Bible is a complex and nuanced text that must be interpreted holistically. Focusing on a few isolated passages while neglecting the overarching themes of love, mercy, and justice leads to a skewed and harmful understanding of God's message. The misuse of Scripture to justify conversion therapy fails to account for the fullness of biblical teaching and the context in which specific passages were written.

- **Twisting Scripture for Harm**: Using the Bible to support conversion therapy often involves twisting Scripture to endorse practices that cause significant psychological, emotional, and spiritual harm. This is contrary to the purpose of Scripture, which is to guide believers in living lives marked by love, healing, and wholeness in Christ. When the Bible is used as a tool for harm, it is being misapplied in a way that betrays its true intent.

The Wrongness of Conversion Therapy

- **Harmful Consequences**: Conversion therapy has been shown to lead to serious negative consequences, including increased rates of depression, anxiety, and suicidal ideation among LGBTQ+ individuals. The Bible teaches that we should care for the well-being of others and avoid causing harm. The misuse of Scripture to justify a practice that results in such profound harm is a violation of this biblical mandate.

- **Violation of Christian Love**: Jesus summarized the law and the prophets with the command to love

God and love one's neighbor as oneself (Matthew 22:37-40). Conversion therapy, which seeks to change an individual's core identity rather than love and accept them as they are, violates this commandment. Using Scripture to justify a lack of love and acceptance is a perversion of the Bible's message.

- **Undermining Human Dignity**: Every person is made in the image of God (Genesis 1:27), and this confers upon them an inherent dignity and worth. Conversion therapy undermines this dignity by suggesting that certain aspects of a person's identity must be changed for them to be acceptable. Misusing the Bible to support this devaluation of human dignity is both inappropriate and contrary to the Christian faith.

The Bible's True Message

- **God's Unconditional Love**: The Bible consistently teaches that God's love is unconditional and not based on a person's ability to conform to human standards. Romans 8:38-39 emphasizes that nothing can separate us from the love of God in Christ Jesus. Misusing Scripture to promote a conditional form of love that requires individuals to change their fundamental identity is a distortion of this biblical truth.

- **Call to Justice and Mercy**: The Bible calls Christians to act justly, love mercy, and walk humbly with

God (Micah 6:8). Conversion therapy, which has been widely condemned by mental health professionals and human rights organizations for its harmful impact, is incompatible with this biblical call to justice and mercy. Using the Bible to justify such a practice is a misuse of Scripture that goes against the values of justice and mercy that are central to the Christian faith.

- **Focus on Healing and Restoration**: Jesus' ministry was characterized by healing and restoration, not by causing harm or division. He reached out to those who were marginalized and oppressed, offering them dignity and love. Conversion therapy, which often results in deep psychological and emotional wounds, is the opposite of the healing and restoration that Jesus exemplified. Using the Bible to justify such harm is a gross misrepresentation of Christ's teachings.

Conclusion

The misuse of biblical texts to justify harm, as seen in the support of conversion therapy, is inappropriate and contrary to the true message of the Bible. Scripture is meant to guide believers toward love, justice, and the affirmation of human dignity. When it is twisted to support practices that inflict harm and deny the worth of individuals, it is being misapplied in ways that betray its core teachings. Christians are called to reject such distortions and to embrace the true spirit of the Bible, which is rooted in unconditional love, compassion, and the pursuit of justice for all people.

7

The belief that "Every person has God-given free will" is central to Christian theology, emphasizing the idea that each individual has the freedom to make choices about their life, including their faith and identity. When this concept is applied to the issue of conversion therapy, it highlights why such practices are fundamentally wrong. Conversion therapy attempts to override an individual's free will by coercing them to change their sexual orientation or gender identity, which contradicts the respect for personal autonomy that is deeply rooted in Christian beliefs.

The Gift of Free Will

- **Biblical Foundation**: The Bible teaches that God created humans with the ability to make choices, a concept known as free will. In Genesis 2:16-17, God gives Adam the choice to obey or disobey His command regarding the tree of the knowledge of good and evil. This gift of free will is a testament to God's respect for human autonomy and the ability to make decisions.

- **Moral Responsibility**: Free will is essential for moral responsibility. Christianity teaches that individuals are accountable for their choices because they have the freedom to choose between right and wrong. This responsibility extends to how one lives their life and expresses their identity. Attempting to force someone to change an intrinsic aspect of their identity through conversion therapy undermines this God-given freedom to live authentically.

The Wrongness of Conversion Therapy

- **Coercion vs. Free Will**: Conversion therapy often involves coercive practices that pressure individuals to change their sexual orientation or gender identity. This coercion violates the principle of free will by attempting to force a person to conform to a particular standard, rather than allowing them to make their own choices about their identity and how they live their life.

- **Denial of Personal Autonomy**: By seeking to change a person's identity, conversion therapy denies the individual's autonomy—their right to decide who they are and how they want to express themselves. This denial of autonomy is a direct contradiction of the respect for free will that is central to Christian ethics. It treats individuals as subjects to be controlled rather than as autonomous beings made in the image of God.

- **Undermining Authenticity**: God-given free will is also about living authentically, making choices that reflect one's true self. Conversion therapy, by attempting to alter a fundamental aspect of a person's identity, undermines the ability to live authentically. It pressures individuals to suppress or change who they are, which is contrary to the freedom God grants to each person to live in accordance with their true nature.

Respecting Free Will in Christian Ethics

- **Following Christ Freely**: In Christianity, following Christ is a choice that must be made freely. Jesus invited people to follow Him, but He never coerced them (Matthew 16:24). This respect for individual choice is central to the Christian faith and should extend to how we approach others, including those whose identities may differ from traditional norms.

- **Love Without Coercion**: True Christian love respects the free will of others. Love that is coerced or forced is not genuine love. Conversion therapy, which often relies on pressure and manipulation, does not reflect the unconditional love that Christians are called to show. Instead, it imposes conditions on acceptance, which is contrary to the way God loves each person unconditionally and allows them the freedom to make their own choices.

- **Promoting Freedom, Not Control**: The Christian message is one of liberation and freedom, not control or domination. Galatians 5:1 states, "It is for freedom that Christ has set us free." This freedom includes the freedom to live in alignment with one's God-given identity. Conversion therapy, by seeking to control or change a person's identity, works against this message of freedom and liberation.

The Christian Call to Affirm Free Will

- **Supporting Individual Journeys**: Christians are called to support others in their personal journeys, recognizing that each person's path is unique and that they must make their own decisions in life. This includes respecting their decisions about their sexual orientation and gender identity. Instead of trying to force change, Christians should offer support, love, and acceptance, trusting that each person's journey is between them and God.

- **Rejecting Coercive Practices**: Because free will is a gift from God, Christians should reject any practice that seeks to coerce or manipulate individuals, including conversion therapy. Such practices not only violate individual autonomy but also go against the Christian principle of loving others as they are, without conditions.

- **Affirming the Image of God in All People**: Respecting free will means recognizing that each person, created in the image of God, has the right to live in a way that reflects their true self. Conversion therapy, which seeks to change this fundamental identity, fails to honor the image of God in each individual. By respecting free will, Christians affirm the dignity and worth of all people as God's creations.

Conclusion

The concept of God-given free will is central to Christian theology and highlights the wrongness of conversion therapy. This practice, which seeks to coerce individuals into changing their sexual orientation or gender identity, violates the respect for personal autonomy and freedom that is foundational to the Christian faith. Instead of trying to control or alter others, Christians are called to respect and affirm the God-given free will of each person, supporting them in their journey with love, compassion, and acceptance.

8

The example of Jesus showing compassion to all, especially marginalized groups, is a cornerstone of Christian ethics and offers a profound critique of the practice of conversion therapy. Throughout the Gospels, Jesus consistently reached out to those who were marginalized, oppressed, and judged by society. His actions and teachings emphasized unconditional love, acceptance, and the dignity of every person, regardless of their social status, identity, or perceived sins. When considering the wrongness of conversion therapy, Jesus' example calls into question any practice that causes harm, marginalizes individuals, or fails to show true compassion.

Jesus' Compassion for the Marginalized

- **Reaching Out to the Outcasts**: Jesus often sought out those whom society had rejected. He ate with tax collectors and sinners (Matthew 9:10-13), spoke with the Samaritan woman at the well (John 4:7-26), and healed lepers who were shunned by the community (Luke 17:11-19). In doing so, Jesus broke social and religious barriers, showing that God's love and compassion extend to everyone, especially those who are marginalized.

- **Affirming Dignity and Worth**: Jesus' interactions with marginalized individuals affirmed their inherent dignity and worth. He treated them with respect, listened to their stories, and offered them healing and hope. This approach starkly contrasts with practices like conversion therapy, which often devalue individuals by suggesting that a core part of their identity needs to be changed or "fixed."

- **Unconditional Love**: Jesus' compassion was rooted in unconditional love—a love that did not require people to change who they were in order to be accepted. His love was freely given, and He invited all to come to Him as they were (Matthew 11:28-30). Conversion therapy, by contrast, often implies that love and acceptance are conditional upon changing one's sexual orientation or gender identity, which contradicts the model of unconditional love that Jesus exemplified.

The Wrongness of Conversion Therapy

- **Marginalizing the Vulnerable**: Conversion therapy targets individuals who are already vulnerable, particularly LGBTQ+ youth, and often subjects them to harmful practices. This marginalization is the opposite of what Jesus demonstrated. Jesus sought to uplift and include the marginalized, not to further isolate or harm them. By subjecting individuals to conversion therapy, we fail to follow Jesus' example of welcoming and caring for those on the margins.

- **Causing Harm, Not Healing**: Jesus' ministry was characterized by healing—both physical and spiritual. He restored sight to the blind, mobility to the paralyzed, and dignity to those who were scorned.

Conversion therapy, on the other hand, has been shown to cause significant psychological and emotional harm, including depression, anxiety, and suicidal thoughts. Such practices are incompatible with the healing ministry of Jesus, who sought to bring wholeness, not harm.

- **Judgment vs. Compassion**: Jesus warned against judging others (Matthew 7:1-2) and instead called His followers to show mercy and compassion. Conversion therapy often stems from a place of judgment, where individuals are viewed as needing to be changed to fit certain norms. This judgmental approach is contrary to the compassion Jesus showed, which did not seek to change people to fit societal expectations but rather embraced them as they were.

Following Jesus' Example of Compassion

- **Embracing Diversity**: Jesus embraced a wide range of people, from different backgrounds and with various struggles. His ministry was inclusive, reflecting the diversity of God's creation. Christians are called to follow this example by embracing and loving people of all sexual orientations and gender identities, recognizing that diversity is a reflection of the richness of God's creation.

- **Supporting the Marginalized**: Just as Jesus defended and uplifted the marginalized, Christians are called to support those who are vulnerable and oppressed. This means rejecting practices like conversion therapy that contribute to marginalization and instead advocating for the dignity, rights, and well-being of LGBTQ+ individuals.

- **Offering True Compassion**: True compassion, as demonstrated by Jesus, involves listening, understanding, and walking alongside others in their struggles. It does not seek to change or judge but to support and love unconditionally. Conversion therapy, which seeks to alter a person's identity, lacks this true compassion and instead imposes a harmful and judgmental agenda.

Conclusion

Jesus' example of showing compassion to all, including marginalized groups, provides a clear model for Christians to follow. Conversion therapy, which causes harm, marginalizes individuals, and fails to offer true compassion, is fundamentally at odds with the teachings and actions of Jesus. As followers of Christ, Christians are called to reject such practices and instead embody the love, acceptance, and compassion that Jesus showed to everyone, especially those who are most vulnerable and marginalized. By doing so, we honor the dignity and worth of every person, following Jesus' command to love others as He has loved us.

9

The rejection of conversion therapy by mainstream medical and psychological communities underscores its wrongness, both ethically and scientifically. Leading health organizations worldwide have denounced conversion therapy as not only ineffective but also harmful, reflecting a broad consensus that aligns with the Christian commitment to love, compassion, and the protection of human dignity.

The Stance of Medical and Psychological Communities

- **Professional Consensus**: Major health organizations, including the American Psychological Association (APA), the American Medical Association (AMA), the World Health Organization (WHO), and the American Academy of Pediatrics (AAP), have unequivocally rejected conversion therapy. These organizations agree that sexual orientation and gender identity are not mental disorders and therefore do not require treatment or change. Their rejection is based on extensive research showing that attempts to change an individual's sexual orientation or gender identity are both ineffective and potentially harmful.

- **Harmful Effects**: Research conducted by these organizations has consistently shown that conversion therapy can lead to significant psychological and emotional harm. This includes increased rates of depression, anxiety, substance abuse, and suicidal thoughts among those who undergo such treatment. The clear consensus from health professionals is that conversion therapy poses a significant risk to mental and emotional well-being, making it a practice that is not only ineffective but dangerous.

- **Ethical Violations**: The mainstream medical and psychological communities also reject conversion therapy on ethical grounds. Forcing or coercing individuals to undergo therapy to change a core aspect of their identity violates principles of autonomy, informed consent, and the commitment to do no harm. Health professionals are ethically bound to respect the dignity and rights of their patients, which includes affirming their identity rather than attempting to change it.

The Wrongness of Conversion Therapy

- **Contradicting Professional Expertise**: The overwhelming rejection of conversion therapy by medical and psychological experts highlights the irresponsibility of supporting or engaging in such practices. From a Christian perspective, ignoring the expert consensus that conversion therapy is harmful contradicts the call to protect and care for others. Just as we trust medical experts in treating physical illnesses, we should also trust their guidance on mental health issues, including the affirmation of LGBTQ+ identities.

- **Causing Harm Contrary to Christian Ethics**: The harm caused by conversion therapy stands in stark contrast to the Christian ethical principle of "do no harm" (Proverbs 3:27). Christianity teaches that we are to love our neighbors and care for their well-being. By participating in or endorsing a practice that is known to cause harm, such as conversion therapy, Christians violate this fundamental ethical obligation.

- **Ignoring Human Dignity**: Conversion therapy undermines the inherent dignity of individuals by treating their sexual orientation or gender identity as something that needs to be fixed or corrected. This perspective is not only unsupported by medical and psychological science but also contradicts the Christian belief that all people are created in the image of God and deserve to be treated with respect and dignity. The rejection of conversion therapy by health professionals reinforces the need to affirm and respect each person's identity.

Alignment with Christian Compassion

- **Affirming Identity and Well-being**: The mainstream medical and psychological communities advocate for the affirmation of LGBTQ+ identities as part of promoting overall mental health and well-being. This aligns with the Christian call to love and support others in their authentic selves. By respecting the findings of health professionals, Christians can better fulfill their duty to care for the emotional and spiritual health of others.

- **Promoting Healing, Not Harm**: Jesus' ministry was centered on healing and restoring individuals to wholeness. The rejection of conversion therapy by health professionals is based on its failure to bring about healing and its tendency to cause harm instead. Christians are called to support practices that lead to genuine healing and reject those that cause suffering, in alignment with the example of Jesus.

- **Following the Science**: The rejection of conversion therapy by mainstream health organizations is grounded in scientific evidence. From a Christian perspective, acknowledging and respecting the truth revealed through science is a way of honoring God's creation. Disregarding the well-established findings of health professionals in favor of harmful practices like conversion therapy is inconsistent with a responsible and compassionate Christian approach.

Conclusion

The rejection of conversion therapy by mainstream medical and psychological communities highlights its inherent wrongness, both ethically and practically. These health professionals, guided by extensive research and a commitment to patient well-being, have found that conversion therapy is not only ineffective but also harmful. From a Christian perspective, respecting this consensus aligns with the core values of love, compassion, and the protection of human dignity. Christians are called to reject harmful practices like conversion therapy and instead embrace approaches that affirm the well-being and identity of all individuals, in keeping with the teachings of Christ and the ethical standards upheld by the medical and psychological communities.

10

Conversion therapy is deeply problematic from a Christian perspective because it induces fear and shame rather than promoting God's love and acceptance. The practice fundamentally contradicts the core Christian teachings of grace, unconditional love, and the inherent worth of every person as created in the image of God. By fostering an environment of fear and shame, conversion therapy alienates individuals from the love of God and distorts the message of the Gospel.

The Role of Fear and Shame in Conversion Therapy

- **Promoting Fear**: Conversion therapy often uses fear as a motivator, suggesting that individuals must change their sexual orientation or gender identity to avoid punishment, rejection, or eternal damnation. This approach instills a deep sense of fear, which can lead to anxiety, self-hatred, and a distorted view of God as punitive rather than loving.

- **Inducing Shame**: The practice of conversion therapy often involves shaming individuals for who they are, labeling their sexual orientation or gender identity as sinful or disordered. This shaming can lead to profound feelings of worthlessness and self-loathing, causing individuals to believe they are fundamentally flawed or unworthy of love. Shame, in this context, becomes a barrier to experiencing God's grace and unconditional love.

- **Contradicting God's Nature**: The God of the Bible is characterized by love, mercy, and acceptance. Scripture tells us that "God is love" (1 John 4:8) and that His perfect love casts out fear (1 John 4:18). By inducing fear and shame, conversion therapy presents a distorted image of God, one that is more focused on judgment and condemnation than on the redemptive love that is at the heart of the Christian faith.

The Wrongness of Conversion Therapy

- **Distorting the Gospel Message**: The Gospel message is one of liberation, grace, and acceptance. Jesus came to offer life in abundance (John 10:10) and to free people from the burdens of sin, guilt, and fear. Conversion therapy, by instilling fear and shame, distorts this message and replaces it with one that is rooted in legalism and conditional acceptance. This is fundamentally at odds with the Gospel, which is about receiving

God's love freely and unconditionally.

- **Alienating Individuals from God**: When individuals are made to feel ashamed of who they are, they may distance themselves from God, believing they are unworthy of His love. This alienation is the opposite of what God desires. Jesus' ministry was about drawing people closer to God, particularly those who felt marginalized or unloved. Conversion therapy, by inducing shame, pushes people away from the very source of love and acceptance they need.

- **Undermining Spiritual Well-being**: Fear and shame are toxic to spiritual well-being. They can lead to a distorted self-image, where individuals view themselves as irreparably broken or sinful. This is contrary to the Christian belief that every person is created in the image of God (Genesis 1:27) and is loved by God just as they are. Conversion therapy undermines this spiritual truth by promoting a narrative of unworthiness and rejection.

Embracing God's Love and Acceptance

- **Unconditional Love**: Christian teaching emphasizes that God's love is unconditional. Romans 8:38-39 assures us that nothing can separate us from the love of God in Christ Jesus. This includes sexual orientation and gender identity. True Christian love reflects God's unconditional love, offering acceptance and support without requiring individuals to change fundamental aspects of who they are.

- **Grace Over Fear**: The Bible repeatedly emphasizes that we are saved by grace, not by our own efforts or conformity to certain standards (Ephesians 2:8-9). This grace is a gift that should lead to freedom and joy, not fear and shame. Conversion therapy, which often operates on the premise that individuals must change to be acceptable, contradicts the concept of grace by implying that God's love is conditional.

- **Healing Through Acceptance**: Jesus' interactions with people were marked by acceptance, healing, and restoration. He welcomed those whom society rejected, offering them love and dignity. For LGBTQ+ individuals, healing and spiritual growth come through acceptance and love, not through coercion or attempts to change their identity. Embracing individuals as they are, without trying to change them, aligns with Jesus' example of compassion and inclusion.

Conclusion

Conversion therapy, by inducing fear and shame, fundamentally misrepresents the nature of God and the message of the Gospel. Instead of fostering a relationship with God based on love, acceptance, and grace, it creates an environment where individuals feel alienated, unworthy, and fearful. This approach is deeply harmful and contradicts the Christian calling to love others as Christ loves us. Christians are called to reject practices like conversion therapy that cause harm and instead embrace an approach that reflects God's unconditional love and acceptance, offering support and compassion to all people, just as they are.

11

Conversion therapy often abuses pastoral or parental authority by exploiting positions of trust and authority to impose harmful practices on individuals, particularly those who are vulnerable. This misuse of authority undermines the principles of respect, care, and ethical responsibility that should guide pastoral and parental relationships. From a Christian perspective, the abuse of such authority in the context of conversion therapy is profoundly wrong for several reasons:

Abuse of Pastoral Authority

- **Misuse of Spiritual Authority**: Pastors and religious leaders are entrusted with guiding their congregants in spiritual matters and providing support. Conversion therapy, however, involves using this spiritual authority to enforce a narrow and harmful view of sexual orientation and gender identity. This misuse of authority undermines the pastoral role, which should be characterized by love, support, and respect for individual dignity.

- **Violation of Trust**: Congregants often look to their pastors for guidance and support during times of personal struggle. Conversion therapy exploits this trust by promoting practices that are not only harmful but also contrary to the principles of compassion and acceptance that should define pastoral care. Such exploitation can lead to significant emotional and spiritual harm, eroding the foundational trust that is essential in any pastoral relationship.

- **Contradiction of Christian Teaching**: Jesus taught that those in positions of leadership should serve others with humility and love (Mark 10:43-45). Conversion therapy, by using pastoral authority to impose change rather than offering unconditional support, contradicts this teaching. Instead of serving others with empathy and respect, it seeks to control and coerce, which is inconsistent with the example of Christ.

Abuse of Parental Authority

- **Coercion and Manipulation**: Parents have a responsibility to guide and support their children, but conversion therapy often involves coercing or manipulating children into changing their sexual orientation or gender identity. This abuse of

parental authority can cause profound
emotional damage, as it forces
children to conform to expectations
that are harmful and deny their true
selves.

- **Denial of Autonomy**: Children
and adolescents are at a stage of
development where they are learning
about their own identities and
gaining independence. Conversion
therapy, by imposing rigid and
harmful expectations, denies young
people the opportunity to explore and
understand their own identities in a
safe and supportive environment.
This denial of autonomy can hinder
their personal and emotional
development and lead to long-term
psychological harm.

- **Erosion of Family Relationships**: When parents impose conversion therapy, it can damage the parent-child relationship, leading to estrangement, conflict, and emotional pain. The parental role should be one of support and unconditional love, but the imposition of harmful practices like conversion therapy can create a dynamic of rejection and control, rather than nurturing and acceptance.

The Wrongness of Conversion Therapy in Context

- **Ethical Responsibility**: Both pastoral and parental authorities have ethical responsibilities to act in the best interests of those they guide or care for. Conversion therapy, by promoting practices that are harmful and discredited, violates these ethical responsibilities. True pastoral and parental care should be based on principles of love, respect, and the well-being of the individual, rather than attempting to control or change them in ways that are damaging.

- **Respect for Human Dignity**: Conversion therapy undermines the inherent dignity of individuals by treating their sexual orientation or gender identity as something that needs to be corrected. This is contrary to the Christian understanding that every person is made in the image of God and deserves to be treated with respect and dignity. Using authority to enforce harmful practices disregards this fundamental respect for human dignity.

- **Alignment with Christian Values**: Christian teachings emphasize love, compassion, and the protection of the vulnerable. Abusing pastoral or parental authority to impose conversion therapy contradicts these values by inflicting harm and causing unnecessary suffering. Christians are called to act with genuine care and empathy, upholding the well-being of others rather than using their positions to enforce harmful and outdated beliefs.

Conclusion

The abuse of pastoral and parental authority in the context of conversion therapy represents a profound violation of trust, respect, and ethical responsibility. By exploiting their positions of power to impose harmful practices, those who support or administer conversion therapy undermine the principles of love, compassion, and dignity that are central to Christian teaching. Instead of using authority to control or coerce, Christians are called to support and affirm individuals in their authentic selves, following the example of Christ's unconditional love and respect for every person.

12

Conversion therapy fundamentally strips individuals of their inherent dignity, a concept deeply rooted in

Christian teachings and ethical principles. By seeking to alter or suppress a core aspect of a person's identity—such as their sexual orientation or gender identity—conversion therapy undermines the respect and value that should be accorded to every human being. This violation of dignity is a significant factor in why conversion therapy is considered profoundly wrong from both a Christian and a human rights perspective.

The Inherent Dignity of Individuals

- **Created in the Image of God**: According to Christian doctrine, every person is created in the image of God (Genesis 1:27). This belief affirms the inherent worth and dignity of every individual, regardless of their sexual orientation or gender identity. The concept of being made in the image of God signifies that every person possesses an intrinsic value and is deserving of respect and honor. Conversion therapy, by attempting to change a fundamental aspect of a person's identity, disregards this divine image and the inherent dignity it represents.

- **Inviolable Worth**: Human dignity is considered inviolable and inalienable. This means that no one has the right to strip another person of their dignity, as it is a fundamental aspect of their humanity. Conversion therapy infringes on this principle by treating a person's sexual orientation or gender identity as something shameful or undesirable that needs to be corrected. This treatment denies the individual's inherent worth and reduces them to a problem to be fixed rather than a person to be respected.

The Wrongness of Conversion Therapy

- **Undermines Self-Acceptance**: Conversion therapy often involves intense pressure for individuals to reject their true selves and conform to heteronormative expectations. This process not only harms mental health but also strips individuals of their ability to accept and love themselves as they are. The promotion of self-rejection and the denial of one's identity is a direct assault on personal dignity, as it negates the worth of the individual as a whole person.

- **Promotes a Deficient View of Human Value**: By framing sexual orientation or gender identity as a problem that needs fixing, conversion therapy promotes a view that these aspects of identity are less valuable or flawed. This perspective is contrary to the Christian understanding that every person is valuable and loved by God just as they are. Such a view undermines the dignity of individuals by suggesting that they are not worthy of love and respect unless they conform to specific norms.

- **Fosters Internalized Shame**: The experience of conversion therapy often results in internalized shame and self-loathing. When individuals are taught to believe that their sexual orientation or gender identity is inherently wrong or sinful, they may internalize these beliefs, leading to significant psychological distress and a diminished sense of self-worth. This internalized shame further erodes their sense of dignity, as they come to view themselves as flawed or unacceptable.

The Christian Call to Uphold Dignity

- **Respect and Compassion**: Christianity teaches that we are to love our neighbors as ourselves

(Mark 12:31) and to show compassion to those who are suffering. Stripping individuals of their dignity through practices like conversion therapy is the antithesis of this call. True Christian love and compassion involve affirming and respecting people for who they are, not subjecting them to harmful practices that deny their inherent worth.

- **Affirmation of True Identity**: Jesus' ministry was marked by an affirmation of people's dignity and worth. He engaged with individuals as they were, showing them respect and offering them healing and acceptance. Conversion therapy's attempts to change people's identities stand in stark contrast to this model, as it disregards their authentic selves and seeks to impose a damaging, externally imposed standard.

- **Advocacy for Human Rights**: The Christian commitment to justice and human rights includes standing against practices that harm individuals and strip them of their dignity. Conversion therapy, which is widely recognized as harmful and dehumanizing, violates these principles. Advocating for the protection and respect of every individual's dignity aligns with Christian teachings on justice and compassion.

Conclusion

Conversion therapy strips individuals of their inherent dignity by attempting to alter or suppress essential aspects of their identity, such as their sexual orientation or gender identity. This approach fundamentally contradicts the Christian understanding of human worth, which holds that every person is created in the image of God and deserving of respect and love. By promoting practices that undermine self-acceptance, propagate shame, and disregard the inherent value of individuals, conversion therapy is profoundly wrong. Christians are called to reject such practices and instead affirm and support individuals in their true identities, honoring their dignity and reflecting

the unconditional love that God has
for all people.

13

Conversion therapy damages trust in
religious communities and leaders by
undermining the very foundations of
faith, support, and pastoral care. This
erosion of trust is a critical aspect of
why conversion therapy is deeply
problematic from a Christian
perspective. The practice not only
harms individuals but also affects the
broader community's perception of
religious institutions and leaders,
leading to significant repercussions
for both individuals and the faith
community as a whole.

Erosion of Trust in Religious Communities

- **Breach of Faith-Based Guidance**: Religious communities often provide a framework of support and guidance based on principles of love, acceptance, and moral integrity. When conversion therapy is endorsed or practiced within these communities, it represents a breach of this foundational trust. Individuals who seek spiritual support may find themselves subjected to harmful practices that contradict the core values of love and compassion, leading to a loss of faith in the community's ability to provide genuine care.

- **Increased Distrust Among LGBTQ+ Individuals**: For LGBTQ+ individuals, experiencing conversion therapy or witnessing its endorsement within a religious context can lead to profound distrust of religious communities. This distrust may stem from the perception that religious institutions prioritize doctrinal conformity over the well-being and dignity of individuals. As a result, LGBTQ+ individuals may feel rejected and alienated, which can drive them away from communities that should ideally be places of acceptance and support.

- **Impact on Community Engagement**: The endorsement of harmful practices like conversion therapy can also affect the wider community's engagement with religious institutions. Potential members who learn of such practices may be deterred from participating in or supporting these communities, seeing them as out of touch or harmful. This can lead to a decline in community cohesion and outreach, impacting the ability of religious organizations to fulfill their mission of service and support.

Damaging Trust in Religious Leaders

- **Abuse of Spiritual Authority**: Religious leaders are entrusted with the role of guiding and nurturing their congregants' spiritual lives. Conversion therapy involves using this authority to enforce harmful practices, which can seriously undermine trust in these leaders. When leaders are perceived as prioritizing doctrinal rigidity over the well-being of individuals, it can lead to a loss of confidence in their ability to provide ethical and compassionate leadership.

- **Perceived Hypocrisy**: Leaders who support or practice conversion therapy may be seen as hypocritical, especially if their actions contradict the teachings of love, acceptance, and respect that are central to Christianity. This perceived hypocrisy can erode the moral authority of religious leaders, causing congregants to question their integrity and commitment to the values they profess.

- **Trauma and Betrayal**:
Individuals who undergo conversion
therapy often experience trauma and
a sense of betrayal, particularly when
such practices are endorsed by
trusted religious leaders. This
betrayal can have long-lasting effects
on their mental and emotional health,
as well as on their perception of
religious leadership. The damage
done to trust in these leaders can be
profound, leading to long-term
disillusionment and estrangement
from the faith community.

The Wrongness of Conversion
Therapy in Relation to Trust

- **Contradiction to Christian
Ethics**: Christian ethics emphasize

the importance of integrity, compassion, and the protection of vulnerable individuals. Conversion therapy, by causing harm and exploiting positions of trust, directly contradicts these ethical principles. Upholding the dignity and well-being of individuals should be paramount, and practices that undermine this are contrary to the essence of Christian teaching.

- **Impact on Pastoral Care**: Effective pastoral care is built on trust and the understanding that leaders act in the best interests of their congregants. Conversion therapy undermines this trust by prioritizing harmful ideologies over the genuine needs of individuals. This erosion of trust can diminish the effectiveness of pastoral care and support, making it more difficult for leaders to fulfill their role as nurturers and guides.

- **Need for Healing and Reconciliation**: The damage done by conversion therapy necessitates efforts toward healing and reconciliation within religious communities. Recognizing the harm caused and working to rebuild trust involves acknowledging past mistakes, providing support to those affected, and committing to practices that align with true Christian values of love and acceptance.

Conclusion

Conversion therapy profoundly damages trust in both religious communities and their leaders by undermining the foundational principles of care, compassion, and ethical integrity. The practice breaches the trust that individuals place in their faith communities and leaders, causing harm and fostering disillusionment. From a Christian perspective, such practices are fundamentally wrong because they contradict the core values of unconditional love and respect for every individual. Rebuilding trust involves rejecting harmful practices, affirming the dignity of all individuals, and ensuring that religious guidance aligns with the true message of the Gospel.

14

Conversion therapy can create significant division and strife within families, exacerbating conflict and harming relationships. From a Christian perspective, this is particularly concerning because the practice undermines the biblical principles of love, unity, and support that should characterize family dynamics. The discord caused by conversion therapy not only affects individual family members but also challenges the integrity and harmony of the family unit as a whole.

How Conversion Therapy Creates Division and Strife

- **Conflict Between Family Members**: Conversion therapy often leads to deep-seated conflict between family members who may have differing views on the practice. Parents who support conversion therapy may impose their beliefs on their LGBTQ+ children, leading to tension and resentment. This conflict can divide families along ideological lines, causing emotional pain and fracturing relationships that should be supportive and nurturing.

- **Emotional Trauma for LGBTQ+ Individuals**: LGBTQ+ individuals subjected to conversion therapy may experience significant emotional trauma, including feelings of rejection, shame, and isolation. This trauma can lead to strained relationships with family members who endorse or are involved in the therapy. The emotional distress caused by these experiences can create long-lasting rifts, making it difficult for families to maintain open and loving relationships.

- **Undermining Family Unity**: The imposition of conversion therapy can disrupt family unity by introducing divisive issues that overshadow the values of love and mutual respect. Families are meant to be places of unconditional support and acceptance, but the presence of conversion therapy can create an environment where differences are highlighted and relationships are strained. This undermines the family's ability to function as a cohesive and supportive unit.

The Wrongness of Conversion Therapy in Relation to Family Dynamics

- **Contradiction to Christian Teachings on Family**: Christian teachings emphasize the importance of love, unity, and support within families. Ephesians 6:1-4, for example, instructs family members to treat each other with respect and understanding. Conversion therapy, by fostering division and conflict, contradicts these teachings. It disrupts the biblical vision of family as a place of unconditional love and mutual support.

- **Emphasis on Compassion and Understanding**: Jesus' teachings emphasize compassion and understanding, particularly towards those who are suffering or marginalized (Matthew 25:40). Conversion therapy often involves coercion and judgment, which are contrary to the compassionate and supportive approach that should define family relationships. The practice of conversion therapy disregards the need for empathy and respect, leading to unnecessary division and strife.

- **Impact on Family Relationships**: The impact of conversion therapy on family relationships can be profound. Families are called to support and nurture each other, providing a foundation of love and security. Conversion therapy disrupts this dynamic by imposing harmful practices that can cause emotional and psychological harm, leading to strained relationships and reduced family cohesion. This undermines the family's role as a source of support and love.

Rebuilding Family Harmony

- **Promoting Acceptance and Support**: To counteract the division caused by conversion therapy, families need to foster an environment of acceptance and support. This involves affirming each family member's identity and well-being, rather than imposing harmful practices that lead to conflict. By focusing on unconditional love and respect, families can work towards healing and rebuilding trust.

- **Open Communication and Understanding**: Addressing the strife created by conversion therapy requires open communication and a willingness to understand each other's perspectives. Families should strive to engage in compassionate and respectful dialogue, aiming to bridge gaps and resolve conflicts in a way that honors each person's dignity and worth.

- **Seeking Reconciliation and Healing**: Reconciliation and healing are crucial for families affected by the divisive effects of conversion therapy. This may involve seeking counseling, engaging in restorative practices, and making a commitment to reject harmful ideologies. By prioritizing reconciliation and the well-being of every family member, families can work towards restoring harmony and unity.

Conclusion

Conversion therapy creates significant division and strife within families, undermining the principles of love, unity, and support that are central to Christian teachings on family relationships. The practice fosters conflict, emotional trauma, and disruption of family cohesion, leading to a breakdown in relationships and trust. From a Christian perspective, this is profoundly wrong because it contradicts the call to love and support one another unconditionally. To address and heal the division caused by conversion therapy, families must focus on acceptance, open communication, and reconciliation, reflecting the values of compassion and understanding that are at the heart of the Christian faith.

15

Conversion therapy fundamentally encourages individuals to live a lie rather than embracing truthfulness, which is at odds with Christian principles of honesty, integrity, and authenticity. This approach involves pressuring individuals to suppress or deny their true selves, leading to a life that is inconsistent with their genuine identity. From a Christian perspective, this is profoundly problematic as it contradicts the call to live in truth and uphold the inherent dignity of every person.

Encouraging a Life of Deception

- **Suppression of Authentic Identity**: Conversion therapy often requires individuals to deny or suppress their sexual orientation or gender identity, compelling them to live inauthentically. This suppression forces individuals to present a façade that is inconsistent with their true selves, leading to a life marked by dishonesty and self-deception. Living in this way can create deep internal conflict and emotional distress, as individuals struggle to reconcile their public persona with their private reality.

- **False Promises of Change**: Conversion therapy promotes the idea that individuals can and should change their sexual orientation or gender identity to align with a particular set of beliefs or norms. This premise is based on the false assumption that such aspects of identity are malleable and inherently wrong. By endorsing these false promises, conversion therapy encourages individuals to live according to a deceptive narrative rather than accepting and embracing their true identity.

- **Compromised Self-Integrity**: The pressure to conform to the expectations set by conversion therapy often results in a compromised sense of self-integrity. Individuals may feel compelled to act in ways that are inconsistent with their own values and experiences, leading to feelings of guilt, shame, and self-betrayal. This internal conflict undermines personal integrity and the ability to live an honest and fulfilling life.

The Wrongness of Conversion Therapy in Relation to Truthfulness

- **Christian Call to Live in Truth**: Christianity teaches the importance of living in truth and being authentic. Jesus said, "You will know the truth, and the truth will set you free" (John 8:32). This call to truthfulness is central to Christian teachings, emphasizing that individuals are called to live in alignment with their true selves and to seek freedom from deception and falsehood. Conversion therapy, by encouraging individuals to live a lie, directly contradicts this call to embrace and live in the truth.

- **Respect for Authentic Identity**: The Christian understanding of human dignity is rooted in the belief that each person is created in the image of God (Genesis 1:27) and that their authentic self is to be respected and valued. Conversion therapy's demand for individuals to change or hide their true identity undermines this respect and fails to honor the intrinsic worth of each person as they are. True Christian love involves accepting and affirming people for who they truly are, not imposing a false identity upon them.

- **Psychological and Spiritual Harm**: Living a lie can have severe psychological and spiritual consequences. The internal conflict and emotional distress caused by conversion therapy can lead to mental health issues, such as depression, anxiety, and diminished self-esteem. Spiritually, it can lead to feelings of estrangement from God and a distorted understanding of one's relationship with the divine. Christianity emphasizes healing, wholeness, and truthfulness, and conversion therapy contradicts these values by fostering harm and deception.

The Path to Authentic Living

- **Embracing True Identity**: The path to authentic living involves accepting and affirming one's true identity rather than trying to conform to external expectations. Christian teachings encourage individuals to embrace their true selves and to find fulfillment in their genuine identity. By doing so, individuals can live more fully and freely, reflecting the divine image in which they were created.

- **Fostering an Environment of Acceptance**: To support individuals in living authentically, Christian communities should foster environments of acceptance and love. This involves rejecting harmful practices like conversion therapy and promoting a message of unconditional acceptance that aligns with the values of truth and integrity. Communities that affirm individuals in their true identity provide a supportive foundation for living an authentic and fulfilling life.

- **Promoting Healing and Reconciliation**: For those affected by conversion therapy, the journey towards healing involves reconciling with their true selves and finding support in their faith community. This process requires acknowledging the harm caused, seeking support, and rebuilding a sense of self-integrity. Christian communities can play a crucial role in this healing process by offering love, acceptance, and encouragement to embrace and live in the truth.

Conclusion

Conversion therapy encourages individuals to live a lie by forcing them to suppress or deny their true sexual orientation or gender identity. This approach fundamentally contradicts Christian teachings on truthfulness, authenticity, and the inherent dignity of every person. Living in truth is central to Christian values, which emphasize the importance of embracing and respecting one's true self. Conversion therapy undermines these principles by promoting deception and self-denial, leading to psychological and spiritual harm. Christians are called to reject such practices and instead support individuals in living authentically, reflecting the love and acceptance that God extends to all people.

16

Conversion therapy can cause individuals to turn away from faith entirely, a profound issue from a Christian perspective. This phenomenon underscores the severe impact that such practices can have on both individuals and their relationship with their faith. The wrongness of conversion therapy is not only evident in its inherent harm but also in how it can drive people away from the very faith that is meant to offer them love, acceptance, and spiritual support.

Impact on Faith and Spiritual Belonging

- **Betrayal of Spiritual Trust**: Individuals who undergo conversion therapy often feel betrayed by the faith communities and leaders they trusted. When religious institutions or leaders endorse or conduct conversion therapy, it can create a profound sense of betrayal. This perceived betrayal can lead individuals to question the integrity and compassion of their faith, making them more likely to distance themselves from the religious community that once supported them.

- **Emotional and Spiritual Trauma**: The emotional and psychological trauma inflicted by conversion therapy can lead to a crisis of faith. Those subjected to these practices may experience profound distress, guilt, and shame, which can erode their sense of spiritual connection and trust in God. This trauma can lead to a rejection of faith altogether, as individuals may come to view religion as a source of pain rather than comfort and guidance.

- **Perceived Incompatibility with Faith**: Conversion therapy often reinforces the belief that one's sexual orientation or gender identity is inherently sinful or wrong. This message can make individuals feel that they are fundamentally incompatible with their faith. The internal conflict between their true selves and the religious expectations imposed upon them can lead to a sense of estrangement from faith, causing them to abandon their beliefs as a way to resolve this conflict.

The Wrongness of Conversion Therapy in Relation to Faith

- **Contradiction to Christian Teachings on Love**: Christianity teaches that God's love is unconditional and that faith should be a source of comfort and acceptance (John 3:16). Conversion therapy, by promoting the idea that certain aspects of a person's identity are unacceptable to God, contradicts this core teaching. The practice can make individuals feel that they are not worthy of God's love, leading them to question or reject their faith.

- **Undermining the Purpose of Faith**: The purpose of faith is to offer guidance, support, and a sense of belonging. Conversion therapy, by inflicting harm and promoting rejection of one's identity, undermines this purpose. Instead of fostering spiritual growth and understanding, it creates a hostile environment that can drive individuals away from their faith. This is contrary to the Christian call to build up and support one another in faith.

- **Impact on Faith Communities**: When faith communities support or engage in conversion therapy, it can damage their reputation and credibility. This not only affects the individuals directly involved but also has broader implications for the community's ability to attract and support others. The harm caused by such practices can lead to a loss of faith among those who feel that their community has betrayed them, weakening the overall spiritual and communal fabric.

Rebuilding Faith and Spiritual Support

- **Promoting Inclusive and Supportive Faith Communities**: To counteract the harm caused by conversion therapy, faith communities need to foster environments that are inclusive, supportive, and affirming of all individuals. This involves rejecting harmful practices and promoting a message of unconditional love and acceptance. By creating spaces where people feel valued and respected, faith communities can help individuals heal and rebuild their connection with their faith.

- **Providing Compassionate Support**: Offering compassionate support to those affected by conversion therapy is crucial in helping them reconnect with their faith. This includes providing pastoral care that affirms their identity and supports their healing process. By addressing the trauma and emotional pain caused by conversion therapy, faith communities can help individuals find solace and reconciliation with their spiritual beliefs.

- **Emphasizing the Core Tenets of Faith**: Reaffirming the core tenets of Christianity, such as love, grace, and acceptance, can help restore faith for those who have been hurt by conversion therapy. Highlighting the inclusive and compassionate aspects of the faith can help individuals see that their true selves are compatible with their spiritual beliefs, fostering a renewed sense of belonging and connection.

Conclusion

Conversion therapy can drive individuals away from faith by causing emotional trauma, creating a sense of betrayal, and fostering a belief that one's true identity is incompatible with religious teachings. This outcome fundamentally undermines the purpose of faith, which is to offer love, support, and a sense of belonging. From a Christian perspective, the practice of conversion therapy is profoundly wrong because it contradicts the teachings of unconditional love and acceptance central to Christianity. To address this issue, faith communities must reject harmful practices, promote inclusive and supportive environments, and emphasize the core values of compassion and grace that align with true Christian teachings.

17

Conversion therapy faces increasing legal restrictions and bans, highlighting growing recognition of its harmful effects and the urgent need to address its ethical and human rights violations. This trend reflects a broader societal and legal consensus that conversion therapy is not only ineffective but also damaging, and it underscores the wrongness of such practices from a legal and ethical standpoint.

Increasing Legal Restrictions and Bans

- **Legislative Action**: Many jurisdictions around the world have enacted laws restricting or outright banning conversion therapy. These legislative measures reflect a growing awareness of the harmful effects of the practice and a commitment to protecting individuals from its detrimental impacts. Laws such as these are often driven by evidence of the psychological and emotional harm caused by conversion therapy, as well as the ethical imperative to safeguard the well-being of vulnerable individuals.

- **Recognition of Harm**: The increasing number of legal restrictions and bans on conversion therapy is based on a broad recognition of the significant harm it causes. Research and testimonials have documented the severe psychological, emotional, and sometimes physical damage resulting from these practices. By imposing legal restrictions, governments and legal systems are acknowledging that conversion therapy is fundamentally harmful and should not be condoned or permitted.

- **Human Rights Considerations**: Legal restrictions and bans on conversion therapy align with the protection of human rights and dignity. The right to be free from torture, inhumane treatment, and discrimination is enshrined in various international human rights agreements and constitutions. Conversion therapy, by inflicting emotional and psychological harm, conflicts with these fundamental human rights principles, prompting legal action to prevent its practice.

The Wrongness of Conversion Therapy in Light of Legal Restrictions

- **Acknowledgement of Harm**: The fact that conversion therapy faces increasing legal restrictions and bans underscores its recognition as harmful and unethical. Laws are enacted to protect individuals from practices deemed damaging or abusive. The legal system's response to conversion therapy reflects an understanding that the practice causes significant harm and violates ethical standards, reinforcing the argument that it is fundamentally wrong.

- **Legal and Ethical Standards**: Legal restrictions on conversion therapy are based on established ethical and professional standards in medicine and psychology. Major medical and psychological organizations, including the American Psychological Association and the World Health Organization, have condemned conversion therapy due to its ineffectiveness and potential for harm. The alignment of legal restrictions with these professional standards highlights the practice's deviation from accepted ethical norms and reinforces its wrongness.

- **Protection of Vulnerable Individuals**: Conversion therapy often targets vulnerable individuals, particularly those who are struggling with their sexual orientation or gender identity. Legal restrictions are designed to protect these individuals from exploitation and harm. The legal system's efforts to ban conversion therapy reflect a commitment to safeguarding those who are most at risk, affirming the principle that ethical practices must prioritize the well-being and dignity of individuals.

Broader Implications and Response

- **Public Awareness and Advocacy**: The legal response to conversion therapy also reflects increasing public awareness and advocacy against the practice. As more people become informed about the harmful effects of conversion therapy, there is growing pressure on legislators and policymakers to take action. This increased awareness contributes to the wrongness of conversion therapy by highlighting its widespread condemnation and the urgent need for reform.

- **Promoting Alternative Approaches**: The trend toward legal restrictions on conversion therapy emphasizes the importance of promoting alternative approaches that affirm and support individuals' identities. Instead of attempting to change a person's sexual orientation or gender identity, ethical and supportive practices focus on acceptance and mental well-being. Legal bans on conversion therapy align with the broader goal of fostering positive and affirming mental health practices.

- **Reinforcement of Ethical Practices**: By instituting legal restrictions and bans on conversion therapy, societies reinforce the importance of adhering to ethical practices that respect individuals' rights and dignity. The legal framework serves to uphold standards of care that align with human rights and psychological well-being, rejecting practices that are proven to be harmful and unethical.

Conclusion

The increasing legal restrictions and bans on conversion therapy reflect a growing recognition of its harmful effects and an acknowledgment of the need to protect individuals from such practices. These legal measures are based on evidence of harm, human rights considerations, and professional ethical standards. The wrongness of conversion therapy is underscored by its alignment with harmful practices that violate the principles of dignity, respect, and ethical treatment. Legal action against conversion therapy not only addresses its damaging impact but also reinforces the commitment to promoting supportive and affirming approaches that honor the true identity and well-being of individuals.

18

Conversion therapy fundamentally fails to celebrate the diversity of God's creation, a key aspect of its wrongness from a Christian perspective. The practice not only rejects but actively seeks to change aspects of individuals' identities that are intrinsic to their being. This stands in stark contrast to the Christian understanding of God's creation, which values and celebrates diversity as a reflection of divine creativity and wisdom.

Failure to Celebrate Divine Diversity

- **Rejection of God's Created Diversity**: Conversion therapy operates under the premise that certain aspects of human diversity, such as sexual orientation or gender identity, are undesirable and need to be altered. This view fundamentally rejects the idea that diversity is a part of God's intentional and beautiful creation. By attempting to change these inherent aspects of identity, conversion therapy disregards the belief that God created each person uniquely and that this diversity reflects His creative power.

- **Incompatibility with Biblical Teachings**: The Bible speaks to the beauty and richness of God's creation. Psalm 139:14 affirms that individuals are "fearfully and wonderfully made," emphasizing that each person is a unique creation of God. Conversion therapy contradicts this teaching by implying that some aspects of a person's identity are not part of God's design or are inherently flawed. This undermines the biblical view that diversity is a positive and integral aspect of creation.

- **Limiting the Scope of God's Creativity**: To endorse conversion therapy is to limit the scope of God's creativity and wisdom. The practice assumes a narrow and exclusionary view of what is acceptable within creation, rejecting the diversity that exists within humanity. This approach fails to recognize that God's creative expression includes a wide range of human experiences and identities, all of which are valuable and deserving of respect.

The Wrongness of Conversion Therapy in Light of Divine Diversity

- **Affirmation of Human Dignity**: Celebrating the diversity of God's creation involves recognizing and affirming the inherent dignity of every person. Conversion therapy, by seeking to change fundamental aspects of a person's identity, undermines this dignity. The Christian understanding of human dignity is rooted in the belief that every individual is made in the image of God (Genesis 1:27) and that this image is reflected in the diversity of human experiences and identities.

- **Christian Call to Love and Acceptance**: Jesus' teachings emphasize love and acceptance for all people, reflecting the inclusive nature of God's creation. In Matthew 22:39, Jesus commands, "Love your neighbor as yourself." This call to love includes embracing and celebrating the diversity among individuals rather than trying to change or diminish it. Conversion therapy, by focusing on altering aspects of identity, contradicts this command and fails to honor the love and acceptance that Jesus espoused.

- **Inclusion and Belonging**: Celebrating diversity is crucial for fostering a sense of inclusion and belonging within faith communities. Conversion therapy creates an environment of exclusion by attempting to force individuals to conform to a specific set of beliefs or norms. This exclusion contradicts the Christian value of welcoming and valuing all people as part of the body of Christ (1 Corinthians 12:12-27), which embraces the full range of human diversity.

Embracing Diversity as a Christian Imperative

- **Promoting an Inclusive Faith Community**: To truly celebrate the diversity of God's creation, faith communities must actively embrace and support individuals of all identities. This involves rejecting practices like conversion therapy and instead fostering an environment where diversity is celebrated as a reflection of God's creative genius. Inclusive communities honor the richness of human experience and the unique ways in which God's image is manifested in each person.

- **Supporting Authenticity and Well-Being**: Embracing diversity means supporting individuals in living authentically and finding fulfillment in their true selves. Conversion therapy undermines this by promoting a harmful agenda of change rather than affirmation. Christian communities are called to support individuals in their journey of self-discovery and acceptance, reflecting the belief that God's creation is diverse and beautifully complex.

- **Advocating for Respect and Understanding**: Celebrating the diversity of God's creation involves advocating for respect and understanding for all people. This includes rejecting harmful practices like conversion therapy and promoting approaches that affirm and support individuals in their diverse identities. By doing so, faith communities can live out the Christian values of love, compassion, and respect for all of God's creation.

Conclusion

Conversion therapy fundamentally fails to celebrate the diversity of God's creation by seeking to alter aspects of individuals' identities that are inherent and valuable. This practice contradicts the Christian understanding of human dignity, the inclusive nature of Jesus' teachings, and the belief that diversity reflects the richness of God's creative work. Embracing and affirming the diversity of all individuals is a central aspect of living out Christian values, and rejecting conversion therapy is a crucial step in honoring and celebrating the full spectrum of God's creation.

19

Conversion therapy is associated with significantly higher rates of suicidal ideation and attempts, which underscores its profound ethical and moral wrongness. From a Christian perspective, this correlation highlights the severe harm caused by conversion therapy and reinforces the imperative to reject practices that endanger individuals' mental and emotional well-being.

Correlation with Suicidal Ideation and Attempts

- **Psychological Distress**: Research has consistently shown that individuals who undergo conversion therapy experience elevated levels of psychological distress, including anxiety, depression, and suicidal thoughts. The pressure to conform to beliefs or expectations that contradict their true identity can lead to intense emotional suffering, contributing to an increased risk of suicidal ideation and attempts. This distress reflects the harmful impact of attempting to change or deny core aspects of one's identity.

- **Rejection and Internalized Shame**: Conversion therapy often involves messages of rejection and shame regarding an individual's sexual orientation or gender identity.

This rejection can cause deep feelings of worthlessness and self-loathing, which are significant risk factors for suicidal thoughts and behaviors. The internalized shame resulting from conversion therapy can lead individuals to believe that their lives are unworthy or unacceptable, heightening the risk of suicide.

- **Lack of Support and Affirmation**: Individuals undergoing conversion therapy may also face a lack of support and affirmation from their faith communities or families. The absence of a supportive network during such a challenging time can exacerbate feelings of isolation and hopelessness. Without adequate emotional support, individuals are more vulnerable to experiencing suicidal ideation and attempts.

The Wrongness of Conversion Therapy in Relation to Mental Health

- **Contradiction to the Christian Call to Care**: Christianity emphasizes the importance of caring for and supporting others, particularly those who are suffering (Matthew 25:35-40). Conversion therapy, by inflicting psychological harm and increasing the risk of suicide, directly contradicts this call to care. Instead of providing support and healing, conversion therapy exacerbates suffering and jeopardizes individuals' mental health.

- **Promotion of Well-being and Healing**: Christian teachings advocate for promoting the well-being and healing of individuals. Practices that harm rather than heal are inconsistent with the principles of compassion and care that are central to the Christian faith. The correlation between conversion therapy and increased rates of suicidal ideation highlights its failure to uphold these principles and its profound ethical wrongness.

- **Moral Responsibility of Faith Communities**: Faith communities have a moral responsibility to protect and support their members. Endorsing or participating in conversion therapy puts individuals at significant risk of mental health crises, including suicidal ideation. The Christian call to protect and nurture life demands rejecting practices that endanger individuals and instead fostering environments that promote mental and emotional well-being.

Addressing the Harm and Promoting Healing

- **Rejecting Harmful Practices**: The link between conversion therapy and higher rates of suicidal ideation underscores the need to reject such practices. Christian communities are called to stand against any practice that causes harm and to advocate for approaches that affirm and support individuals in their true identities. By rejecting conversion therapy, faith communities align with the principles of compassion, respect, and support.

- **Providing Supportive Alternatives**: To address the harm caused by conversion therapy, faith communities should focus on providing supportive and affirming alternatives. This includes offering counseling and pastoral care that promote mental health and well-being without attempting to change fundamental aspects of a person's identity. Supportive environments help individuals feel valued and accepted, reducing the risk of mental health crises and fostering a sense of belonging.

- **Advocating for Mental Health**: Promoting mental health and well-being is essential for preventing the severe outcomes associated with conversion therapy. Christian communities should advocate for mental health resources and support systems that are affirming and respectful of individuals' identities. By prioritizing mental health and providing affirming support, communities can help mitigate the risk of suicidal ideation and foster overall well-being.

Conclusion

The correlation between conversion therapy and higher rates of suicidal ideation and attempts highlights its profound wrongness from both an ethical and Christian perspective. Conversion therapy inflicts significant psychological harm, contradicting the Christian call to care for and support others. Rejecting conversion therapy and promoting supportive, affirming approaches are essential for protecting individuals' mental health and well-being. By doing so, faith communities can uphold the values of compassion, respect, and life-affirming care that are central to Christian teachings.

20

Conversion therapy often involves coercion and a lack of true consent, which underscores its profound ethical and moral wrongness. This practice not only infringes on individual autonomy but also exploits vulnerabilities, making it a deeply harmful and unethical approach from both a psychological and Christian perspective.

Coercion and Lack of True Consent in Conversion Therapy

- **Pressure and Manipulation**: Conversion therapy frequently involves significant pressure and manipulation, particularly from religious leaders, family members, or therapists who hold significant influence over the individual. This coercion can create an environment where individuals feel compelled to participate in therapy, not out of genuine desire or belief in its efficacy, but because of external pressures. Such coercion undermines the concept of true consent, which requires that individuals make decisions freely and without undue influence.

- **Exploitation of Vulnerability**: Individuals who undergo conversion therapy are often in vulnerable positions, struggling with their identity or seeking acceptance from their faith communities. This vulnerability can be exploited by those promoting conversion therapy, who may promise spiritual or emotional rewards in exchange for compliance. This exploitation further compromises the authenticity of consent, as individuals may agree to participate not because they truly want to, but because they are seeking relief from their distress or acceptance from their community.

- **Lack of Informed Consent**: True consent requires that individuals are fully informed about the potential risks and outcomes of the therapy they are undergoing. Conversion therapy often fails to provide accurate information about the practice's ineffectiveness and potential for harm. Without comprehensive and truthful information, individuals cannot give fully informed consent, making the practice fundamentally unethical. The lack of transparency and informed consent is a significant issue that highlights the wrongness of conversion therapy.

The Wrongness of Conversion Therapy in Light of Coercion and Consent

- **Violation of Personal Autonomy**: True consent is grounded in respect for personal autonomy and the ability to make decisions free from coercion. Conversion therapy, by involving manipulation and pressure, violates this principle. Individuals subjected to conversion therapy are often denied the opportunity to make autonomous decisions about their own identities and well-being. This infringement on personal autonomy is a significant ethical issue, as it disregards the fundamental rights and dignity of individuals.

- **Ethical Implications for Christian Communities**: Christianity teaches the importance of respecting and honoring each person's dignity and autonomy. Coercive practices that undermine an individual's ability to make free and informed choices are inconsistent with these teachings. Jesus' command to love and respect others (Matthew 22:39) implies that individuals should be treated with honor and integrity, which includes respecting their freedom to make choices about their own lives. Conversion therapy's coercive nature contradicts this call to respect and care.

- **Moral Responsibility of Faith Leaders**: Faith leaders and communities have a moral responsibility to support and affirm individuals, not to coerce or manipulate them into conforming to specific beliefs or practices. The use of coercion in conversion therapy undermines the trust and ethical responsibility that faith leaders are called to uphold. By engaging in or endorsing conversion therapy, leaders betray their role as guides and supporters, contributing to harm rather than healing.

Addressing Coercion and Promoting Genuine Consent

- **Promoting Ethical Practices**: To address the issue of coercion and lack of true consent, it is essential to promote ethical practices that respect individual autonomy and dignity.

This involves rejecting conversion therapy and advocating for approaches that prioritize informed consent and respect for personal identity. Ethical practices in therapy and counseling should be transparent, consensual, and free from undue influence or pressure.

- **Creating Supportive Environments**: Faith communities should focus on creating supportive and affirming environments where individuals can make decisions about their identities and well-being without fear of coercion. This includes offering support and acceptance rather than attempting to change individuals' identities. By fostering environments that respect and honor personal autonomy, communities can help ensure that individuals make choices that are genuinely reflective of their own values and beliefs.

- **Providing Accurate Information and Resources**: Ensuring that individuals have access to accurate information about the potential risks and outcomes of any therapy is crucial for maintaining true consent. This includes educating individuals about the ineffectiveness and harm associated with conversion therapy, so they can make informed decisions about their own mental health and well-being. Transparency and access to reliable resources are essential for upholding ethical standards and respecting personal autonomy.

Conclusion

The coercive nature of conversion therapy and the lack of true consent it involves underscore its profound ethical and moral wrongness. By undermining personal autonomy and exploiting vulnerabilities, conversion therapy fails to respect the dignity and rights of individuals. From a Christian perspective, this practice contradicts the values of respect, love, and ethical care that are central to the faith. Addressing these issues requires rejecting conversion therapy, promoting ethical practices, and creating supportive environments that honor individuals' autonomy and provide accurate information.

21

Conversion therapy breeds hostility rather than Christian fellowship, highlighting its profound ethical and moral wrongness. This practice undermines the core values of love, unity, and mutual respect that are central to Christian teachings, instead fostering division and conflict within communities.

Breeding Hostility Instead of Christian Fellowship

- **Fostering Division and Conflict**: Conversion therapy often creates a divisive atmosphere within faith communities by promoting the idea that certain identities or orientations are unacceptable. This can lead to significant internal conflict, as individuals are pitted against one another based on their personal identities. The focus on changing or rejecting aspects of identity contributes to an environment of hostility and disagreement, rather than fostering a sense of unity and fellowship.

- **Creating an Us vs. Them Mentality**: The very premise of conversion therapy implies that those who do not conform to certain religious expectations are somehow inferior or flawed. This can foster an "us vs. them" mentality, where individuals who are subject to conversion therapy feel marginalized and alienated from their faith communities. Such an environment is antithetical to the Christian call for inclusivity and mutual support, breeding hostility rather than genuine fellowship.

- **Undermining Trust and Respect**: Conversion therapy can undermine trust and respect within faith communities by promoting harmful and judgmental attitudes. When individuals are coerced or pressured to change aspects of their identity, it erodes the trust they have in their community and its leaders. This lack of trust and respect is detrimental to the spirit of Christian fellowship, which is built on mutual support, understanding, and compassion.

The Wrongness of Conversion Therapy in Relation to Christian Fellowship

- **Contradiction to Christian Teachings on Love and Unity**: Christianity emphasizes the importance of love, unity, and fellowship among believers (John 13:34-35; 1 Corinthians 1:10). Conversion therapy, by creating an environment of rejection and division, contradicts these fundamental teachings. Instead of promoting a loving and inclusive community, it fosters an atmosphere of hostility and exclusion, which is contrary to the principles of Christian fellowship.

- **Promoting Compassion and Acceptance**: Jesus' teachings call for compassion and acceptance, encouraging believers to embrace and support one another (Matthew 25:35-40; Galatians 6:2). Conversion therapy's focus on changing individuals rather than supporting them in their true selves is at odds with this call. The practice undermines the Christian mandate to show kindness and acceptance, replacing it with a focus on judgment and rejection.

- **Building a Supportive Community**: True Christian fellowship is characterized by a supportive and affirming community where individuals are encouraged to grow in their faith and identity.

Conversion therapy disrupts this by creating a hostile environment that is not conducive to spiritual growth or personal well-being. By rejecting the practice and promoting supportive and inclusive practices, faith communities can build a stronger, more united fellowship that aligns with Christian values.

Addressing Hostility and Fostering Genuine Fellowship

- **Embracing Inclusivity and Respect**: To counteract the hostility bred by conversion therapy, faith communities should embrace inclusivity and respect for all individuals. This involves rejecting practices that create division and instead fostering an environment where everyone feels valued and accepted. By promoting inclusivity, communities can build stronger bonds of fellowship and mutual support.

- **Encouraging Open Dialogue and Understanding**: Open dialogue and understanding are crucial for building Christian fellowship. Creating spaces where individuals can openly discuss their experiences and concerns without fear of judgment or rejection helps to build trust and strengthen community bonds. This approach contrasts sharply with the divisive nature of conversion therapy, promoting instead a spirit of unity and mutual respect.

- **Supporting Affirming Practices**: Faith communities should focus on affirming practices that support individuals in their authentic identities. This includes offering pastoral care and counseling that respect and value individuals as they are, rather than attempting to change them. Affirming practices help to create a supportive environment that aligns with Christian teachings on love and fellowship.

Conclusion

Conversion therapy breeds hostility rather than Christian fellowship, fundamentally undermining the values of love, unity, and mutual respect central to Christian teachings.

By creating division, fostering an "us vs. them" mentality, and undermining trust and respect, conversion therapy contradicts the principles of genuine Christian fellowship. Addressing the wrongness of conversion therapy involves rejecting its divisive nature and promoting inclusivity, open dialogue, and affirming practices that build a supportive and loving community. By doing so, faith communities can uphold the true spirit of Christian fellowship and reflect the love and acceptance that are central to their beliefs.

22

Conversion therapy stands in stark contrast to Jesus' approach of ministering to the marginalized rather than condemning them. Jesus' ministry was characterized by compassion, acceptance, and a commitment to uplifting those who were marginalized or rejected by society. Conversion therapy, in its attempt to alter fundamental aspects of individuals' identities, fundamentally contradicts this model of love and inclusion.

Jesus' Ministry to the Marginalized

- **Compassionate Engagement**: Jesus consistently engaged with individuals who were marginalized or ostracized by society. He reached out to tax collectors, sinners, the sick, and those considered unclean, offering them compassion and acceptance rather than condemnation (Matthew 9:10-13; Luke 5:12-13). His approach was one of healing and inclusion, affirming their worth and dignity rather than seeking to change or reject them.

- **Emphasis on Love and Acceptance**: Jesus' interactions with marginalized individuals were marked by love and acceptance. He did not condemn or judge them for their social status or personal struggles but instead offered them grace and understanding. For instance, His encounter with the woman at the well (John 4:1-26) demonstrates His willingness to break societal norms and offer acceptance to someone who was socially marginalized.

- **Call to Support the Marginalized**: Jesus taught His followers to care for and support the marginalized, reflecting His own ministry. In Matthew 25:35-40, Jesus emphasizes the importance of serving those in need, stating that such acts of kindness are akin to serving Him. This teaching underscores the call to uplift and support the marginalized rather than seeking to change or condemn them.

The Wrongness of Conversion Therapy in Light of Jesus' Ministry

- **Contradiction to Compassionate Care**: Conversion therapy is fundamentally opposed to the compassionate care exemplified by Jesus. Instead of offering acceptance and understanding, conversion therapy seeks to alter essential aspects of individuals' identities, often through coercive and harmful methods. This approach is contrary to the compassion and respect that Jesus modeled in His ministry.

- **Promotion of Exclusion Rather Than Inclusion**: Jesus' ministry was characterized by inclusion and the breaking down of barriers that separated people from God's love. Conversion therapy, however, promotes exclusion by suggesting that certain identities or orientations are unacceptable or flawed. This exclusionary approach contradicts

Jesus' example of welcoming and affirming those who were marginalized.

- **Undermining Dignity and Worth**: Conversion therapy undermines the inherent dignity and worth of individuals by implying that their identities are inherently flawed or in need of change. This is in direct opposition to Jesus' ministry, which affirmed the dignity and worth of every person. By seeking to change individuals rather than affirming their intrinsic value, conversion therapy disregards the message of love and respect that Jesus demonstrated.

Embracing Jesus' Model in Christian Communities

- **Affirming Identity and Worth**: Following Jesus' example involves affirming the identities and worth of all individuals, rather than seeking to change them. Faith communities should embrace and support individuals in their authentic selves, reflecting Jesus' approach of acceptance and love. This involves creating environments where people feel valued and supported, in alignment with the compassionate and inclusive ministry of Jesus.

- **Offering Support and Healing**: Just as Jesus offered healing and support to those who were marginalized, Christian communities should focus on providing supportive and affirming care. This means rejecting practices like conversion therapy that cause harm and instead promoting approaches that respect and nurture individuals' true identities. Offering support and healing aligns with the values demonstrated by Jesus in His ministry.

- **Advocating for Justice and Inclusion**: Embracing Jesus' ministry involves advocating for justice and inclusion for marginalized individuals. This includes standing against harmful practices such as conversion therapy and promoting policies and practices that reflect Jesus' teachings on love and acceptance. By advocating for justice and inclusion, faith communities can live out the principles of compassion and respect that are central to Jesus' message.

Conclusion

Conversion therapy is fundamentally at odds with Jesus' approach of ministering to the marginalized. While Jesus reached out with compassion, acceptance, and a commitment to inclusivity, conversion therapy seeks to alter and condemn aspects of individuals' identities, causing harm and division. Embracing Jesus' model of ministry involves affirming the worth and dignity of all individuals, offering support and healing, and advocating for justice and inclusion. By rejecting conversion therapy and promoting practices that reflect Jesus' love and acceptance, faith communities can more fully embody the principles of compassion and inclusion that are central to His teachings.

23

Conversion therapy fundamentally contradicts the inclusive nature of Christ's message, which is central to the Christian faith. Jesus' teachings and actions consistently exemplify inclusivity, compassion, and acceptance, embracing individuals from all walks of life without judgment or exclusion. Conversion therapy, by attempting to change or reject fundamental aspects of a person's identity, directly opposes these core elements of Christ's message.

The Inclusive Nature of Christ's Message

- **Embracing All People**: Jesus' ministry was marked by His outreach to individuals who were marginalized or rejected by society, including tax collectors, sinners, and those deemed unclean (Matthew 9:10-13; Luke 19:1-10). He extended His love and acceptance to all people, regardless of their social status or personal struggles. This inclusivity reflects the essence of Christ's message, which emphasizes that everyone is worthy of God's love and grace.

- **Breaking Down Barriers**: Jesus consistently broke down societal and cultural barriers that divided people.

For example, His interactions with women, Gentiles, and Samaritans challenged prevailing norms and demonstrated His commitment to inclusivity (John 4:1-30; Mark 7:24-30). By transcending these barriers, Jesus illustrated that God's love is available to everyone, regardless of societal divisions.

- **Call to Love and Acceptance**: Jesus taught His followers to love their neighbors as themselves and to show compassion and kindness to others (Matthew 22:39; Luke 10:25-37). His parables, such as the Good Samaritan, emphasize the importance of loving and accepting others beyond conventional boundaries (Luke 10:30-37). This call to love and acceptance underscores the inclusive nature of Christ's message.

The Wrongness of Conversion Therapy in Light of Christ's Inclusivity

- **Exclusionary Practice**: Conversion therapy operates on the premise that certain identities or orientations are unacceptable or flawed and need to be changed. This approach is fundamentally exclusionary, suggesting that individuals who do not conform to specific religious or societal expectations are unworthy or defective. This exclusion contradicts the inclusive nature of Christ's message, which affirms the worth and dignity of all people.

- **Undermining the Value of Individuals**: By seeking to alter core aspects of an individual's identity, conversion therapy undermines their inherent value and worth as created by God. This stands in stark contrast to Christ's message, which affirms the intrinsic value of every person and emphasizes that all are made in the image of God (Genesis 1:27). Conversion therapy's focus on changing people rather than accepting them as they are fails to reflect the inclusive and affirming nature of Christ's teachings.

- **Promoting Division Rather Than Unity**: Conversion therapy can create division and conflict within communities by positioning certain identities as problematic or in need of correction. This division contradicts Christ's message of unity and reconciliation, which calls for bringing people together in love and understanding (John 17:20-23; Ephesians 4:3). Instead of fostering unity, conversion therapy fosters discord and separation.

Reflecting Christ's Message in Christian Communities

- **Embracing Diversity and Inclusion**: To align with the inclusive nature of Christ's message, faith communities should embrace and celebrate diversity rather than seeking to change or reject individuals based on their identities. This involves creating welcoming environments where all individuals are valued and supported, reflecting Christ's teachings of acceptance and love.

- **Supporting Authenticity**: Reflecting Christ's message means supporting individuals in their authentic identities rather than imposing restrictive norms. By affirming individuals as they are, faith communities honor the inclusivity that Christ exemplified. This support fosters a sense of belonging and reinforces the message of unconditional love and acceptance.

- **Advocating for Compassion and Understanding**: Faith communities should advocate for compassion and understanding, rejecting practices like conversion therapy that are contrary to the inclusive nature of Christ's message. Promoting compassionate and supportive approaches aligns with Jesus' teachings and helps build a community rooted in love and acceptance.

Conclusion

Conversion therapy fundamentally contradicts the inclusive nature of Christ's message by promoting exclusion, division, and the rejection of individuals based on their identities. Jesus' ministry was characterized by compassion, acceptance, and the breaking down of societal barriers, embracing all

people without judgment. To uphold
the essence of Christ's teachings,
faith communities must reject
conversion therapy and instead foster
environments of inclusivity, support,
and unconditional love. By doing so,
they reflect the true spirit of Christ's
message and honor the inherent
worth and dignity of every
individual.

24

Conversion therapy neglects the Holy
Spirit's guidance in individual lives,
highlighting its fundamental ethical
and theological shortcomings. The
Holy Spirit plays a crucial role in
guiding, comforting, and affirming
believers, helping them navigate their
spiritual journeys with authenticity

and grace. Conversion therapy, by attempting to alter core aspects of an individual's identity, disregards this divine guidance and undermines the process of personal spiritual growth.

The Role of the Holy Spirit in Individual Lives

- **Guidance and Comfort**: The Holy Spirit is described in Scripture as a guide and comforter who leads believers into all truth and provides them with the strength and assurance they need (John 14:16-17, 26; John 16:13). This guidance is integral to understanding one's identity and relationship with God. The Spirit works within individuals to reveal God's love and purpose for their lives, offering support and wisdom in their personal and spiritual journeys.

- **Affirmation and Validation**: The Holy Spirit also affirms the inherent worth and value of each individual as a child of God. This affirmation is crucial for spiritual health and personal well-being, providing a sense of belonging and purpose. The Spirit's work involves nurturing individuals' understanding of their true selves in light of God's love and acceptance, rather than imposing external standards or expectations.

- **Empowerment for Authentic Living**: The Holy Spirit empowers believers to live authentically according to their God-given identities and callings. This empowerment includes providing the courage to embrace one's true self and to live in alignment with God's will. The Spirit encourages individuals to grow in their understanding of themselves and their relationship with God, fostering an environment where personal authenticity is celebrated.

The Wrongness of Conversion Therapy in Relation to the Holy Spirit's Guidance

- **Disregarding Divine Guidance**: Conversion therapy disregards the Holy Spirit's role in guiding individuals by imposing external standards or attempting to change fundamental aspects of their identity. This approach contradicts the Spirit's work, which involves guiding individuals to understand and embrace their authentic selves. Conversion therapy assumes that the Spirit's guidance is insufficient or incorrect, undermining the Spirit's role in the believer's life.

- **Contradicting Spiritual Affirmation**: The Holy Spirit affirms each person's identity as part of God's creation. Conversion therapy, by seeking to alter or correct aspects of a person's identity, negates this divine affirmation. It implies that individuals need to change to be acceptable to God, rather than recognizing and embracing their worth as affirmed by the Spirit.

- **Imposing External Standards**: Conversion therapy imposes external standards of what is deemed acceptable, rather than allowing the Holy Spirit to guide individuals in their personal spiritual journeys. This imposition can lead to a conflict between the individual's true self and the expectations imposed upon them, causing spiritual distress and hindering personal growth. It fails to respect the Spirit's role in shaping each person's unique path in their relationship with God.

Upholding the Role of the Holy Spirit in Christian Communities

- **Respecting Individual Guidance**: Faith communities should respect and support the guidance of the Holy Spirit in each individual's life. This involves trusting that the Spirit works within people to reveal their true selves and to guide them in their spiritual journeys. Rejecting practices like conversion therapy and promoting approaches that honor the Spirit's work align with this respect for divine guidance.

- **Encouraging Authentic Spiritual Growth**: Supporting individuals in their authentic identities allows them to grow spiritually in harmony with the Holy Spirit's guidance. This means fostering environments where people can explore and understand their relationship with God without the pressure to conform to external expectations. Encouraging authentic spiritual growth aligns with the Spirit's role in guiding and affirming individuals.

- **Promoting Supportive and Affirming Practices**: Christian communities should promote supportive and affirming practices that align with the Holy Spirit's work. This includes providing pastoral care and counseling that respects and nurtures individuals' authentic identities rather than attempting to change them. Such practices honor the Spirit's guidance and support individuals in their journey of faith.

Conclusion

Conversion therapy neglects the Holy Spirit's guidance by imposing external standards and attempting to change fundamental aspects of an individual's identity. The Holy Spirit's role in guiding, affirming, and empowering believers is crucial for their spiritual well-being and authenticity. By disregarding the Spirit's work, conversion therapy undermines the divine guidance that is essential for personal and spiritual growth. Faith communities should reject conversion therapy and instead support practices that honor and align with the Holy Spirit's role in each individual's life, fostering environments where people can grow authentically in their relationship with God.

25

Conversion therapy can significantly worsen depression and anxiety, illustrating its profound ethical and psychological wrongness. This practice, which aims to change an individual's sexual orientation or gender identity through various methods, often exacerbates mental health issues rather than providing the support and healing it claims to offer.

The Impact of Conversion Therapy on Mental Health

- **Increased Depression**: Studies and testimonies from those who have undergone conversion therapy frequently reveal a rise in depressive symptoms. The practice often leads to feelings of inadequacy, self-loathing, and hopelessness as individuals are pressured to change fundamental aspects of who they are. The dissonance between their true identity and the external pressures to conform can deepen feelings of depression and emotional distress.

- **Heightened Anxiety**: Conversion therapy can significantly increase anxiety levels. The constant pressure to conform to imposed norms or expectations creates a high-stress environment. Individuals may experience chronic anxiety due to fear of failure, rejection, or punishment for not meeting the therapy's demands. This ongoing stress contributes to heightened anxiety and can lead to severe emotional turmoil.

- **Self-Esteem and Identity Issues**: Conversion therapy often damages self-esteem by reinforcing negative self-beliefs. When individuals are told that their identity is flawed or in need of change, it undermines their self-worth and contributes to a distorted self-image. This can result in long-term issues with self-esteem and identity, exacerbating both depression and anxiety.

The Wrongness of Conversion Therapy in Light of Mental Health Concerns

- **Contradicts Ethical Care Principles**: Ethical care practices prioritize the well-being and mental health of individuals, focusing on support, acceptance, and effective interventions. Conversion therapy, by worsening depression and anxiety, contradicts these principles and fails to provide the compassionate and respectful care that individuals deserve. Its harmful impact on mental health demonstrates a fundamental disregard for the ethical duty to promote well-being.

- **Lack of Efficacy and Harm**: The ineffectiveness of conversion therapy in achieving its goals is well-documented, while its harmful effects on mental health are widely recognized. The American

Psychological Association, the World Health Organization, and other major health organizations condemn conversion therapy due to its lack of scientific support and its documented harm, including increased rates of depression and anxiety. This evidence highlights the wrongness of continuing such practices.

- **Violation of Dignity and Respect**: Conversion therapy violates the dignity and respect that every individual deserves. By attempting to alter fundamental aspects of a person's identity and inflicting emotional distress, it disregards their inherent worth and humanity. This disregard is antithetical to ethical care practices and the respect that should be afforded to all individuals, reinforcing the wrongness of conversion therapy.

Addressing Mental Health Concerns and Promoting Well-Being

- **Supporting Mental Health**: To address the mental health issues associated with conversion therapy, it is crucial to support individuals through affirming and respectful practices. This includes offering counseling and care that acknowledges and validates their identities, rather than attempting to change them. Supportive approaches help improve mental health and well-being, aligning with ethical care principles.

- **Advocating for Evidence-Based Practices**: Faith communities and mental health professionals should advocate for evidence-based practices that promote mental health and well-being. This includes rejecting conversion therapy and supporting approaches that are backed by scientific research and ethical standards. Evidence-based practices focus on providing effective and compassionate care that respects individuals' identities and supports their mental health.

- **Creating Affirming Environments**: Creating environments that affirm individuals' identities and provide supportive care is essential for mental health. This involves fostering acceptance and understanding within faith communities and mental health settings, ensuring that individuals feel valued and supported. Affirming environments contribute to improved mental health outcomes and help counteract the harmful effects of practices like conversion therapy.

Conclusion

Conversion therapy can significantly worsen depression and anxiety, demonstrating its profound ethical and psychological wrongness. By exacerbating mental health issues and failing to provide effective support, conversion therapy contradicts the principles of ethical care and respect for individuals' dignity. Addressing these issues involves rejecting conversion therapy and promoting affirming, evidence-based practices that support mental health and well-being. By fostering supportive environments and advocating for ethical care, faith communities and mental health professionals can uphold the dignity and respect that every individual deserves.

26

Conversion therapy is fundamentally flawed as it suggests false hope of "change" without any credible evidence to support its effectiveness. This practice promises to alter an individual's sexual orientation or gender identity, yet lacks scientific validation and often leads to significant emotional and psychological harm. The wrongness of conversion therapy is underscored by its provision of misleading assurances and its disregard for empirical evidence.

The Illusion of 'Change' Promised by Conversion Therapy

- **Lack of Scientific Evidence**: Conversion therapy promises to change an individual's sexual orientation or gender identity, but there is no scientific evidence to support these claims. Major medical and psychological organizations, including the American Psychological Association, the World Health Organization, and the National Association of Social Workers, have denounced conversion therapy as ineffective and harmful. This lack of evidence highlights the deceptive nature of the therapy's promises and exposes it as a misguided and unethical practice.

- **Misleading Expectations**: Conversion therapy often creates unrealistic expectations of change, leading individuals to believe that their core identity can be altered. This promise of transformation can result in prolonged and distressing efforts to achieve an unattainable goal. The failure to produce the promised results can deepen feelings of inadequacy, guilt, and self-blame, contributing to emotional distress and psychological harm.

- **Reinforcing Harmful Beliefs**: By suggesting that one's sexual orientation or gender identity is something that needs to be changed, conversion therapy reinforces harmful and stigmatizing beliefs. It perpetuates the notion that there is something inherently wrong with individuals who do not conform to specific norms, further marginalizing and invalidating their identities. This reinforcement of negative beliefs contradicts the principles of dignity and respect that are essential to ethical care.

The Wrongness of Conversion Therapy in Relation to False Hope

- **Ethical Violations**: Conversion therapy's promise of change without evidence represents a serious ethical violation. Ethical care practices are grounded in honesty, evidence-based approaches, and respect for individuals' well-being. Conversion therapy's deceptive promises and lack of scientific support undermine these ethical principles, leading to significant harm and disillusionment among those who undergo the therapy.

- **Psychological Harm**: The false hope of change promoted by conversion therapy can cause significant psychological harm. Individuals who are led to believe that their identity can be altered may experience ongoing emotional distress and mental health issues when they are unable to meet these unrealistic expectations. This harm underscores the wrongness of conversion therapy and highlights the need for approaches that are grounded in evidence and respect for individual identities.

- **Undermining Trust**: The promises made by conversion therapy can undermine trust in mental health professionals, faith communities, and institutions that support individuals. When the therapy fails to deliver on its promises, it can lead to a loss of trust and faith in these systems, further exacerbating feelings of isolation and distress. This breach of trust is another significant ethical concern associated with conversion therapy.

Promoting Evidence-Based and Respectful Approaches

- **Advocating for Evidence-Based Practices**: To counteract the wrongness of conversion therapy, it is essential to advocate for evidence-based practices that are supported by scientific research and ethical standards. This includes providing mental health care and counseling that respects and affirms individuals' identities without promising unrealistic or unproven outcomes.

- **Fostering Honest Communication**: Ensuring that individuals receive honest and transparent information about mental health care options is crucial. This involves communicating the limits of what therapy can achieve and focusing on support and affirmation rather than false promises. Honest communication helps to build trust and ensures that individuals are not misled by unfounded claims.

- **Supporting Affirmation and Respect**: Providing support that respects and affirms individuals' identities, rather than attempting to change them, aligns with ethical care principles and promotes well-being. This approach acknowledges the inherent worth of each person and supports their mental health in a manner that is consistent with evidence-based practices.

Conclusion

Conversion therapy's suggestion of false hope for "change" without evidence is a fundamental ethical and psychological failing. By promising outcomes that lack scientific support and often lead to significant harm, conversion therapy violates principles of honesty, respect, and evidence-based care. Addressing the wrongness of conversion therapy involves promoting evidence-based practices, fostering honest communication, and supporting affirming approaches that respect individuals' identities. By rejecting conversion therapy and focusing on ethical and respectful care, faith communities and mental health professionals can uphold the dignity and well-being of all individuals.

Conversion therapy profoundly harms the witness of the Church to the wider world, undermining its credibility and its mission to exemplify love, compassion, and truth. The practice of conversion therapy, with its unsubstantiated claims and damaging effects, contradicts the core values of the Christian faith and tarnishes the Church's ability to effectively communicate the gospel message.

The Impact of Conversion Therapy on the Church's Witness

- **Contradiction to Christian Love and Compassion**: Conversion therapy stands in stark contrast to the

Christian call to love and compassion. Jesus taught His followers to love their neighbors as themselves (Mark 12:31) and to offer grace and acceptance to all people. The harmful nature of conversion therapy, which often involves coercion and emotional distress, directly contradicts this fundamental teaching. By endorsing or participating in such practices, the Church undermines its own message of unconditional love and acceptance.

- **Damage to Church Credibility**: The use of conversion therapy damages the credibility of the Church in the eyes of the wider world. When the Church is associated with practices that are widely condemned by mental health professionals and human rights organizations, it risks losing its moral authority and influence. This erosion of credibility can hinder the Church's ability to effectively share its message and engage meaningfully with society.

- **Misrepresentation of Christian Values**: Conversion therapy can misrepresent Christian values by associating the faith with harmful practices and exclusionary attitudes. This misrepresentation can create a negative perception of Christianity as being intolerant or judgmental, rather than as a faith characterized by inclusivity, compassion, and respect for the inherent worth of every individual.

The Wrongness of Conversion Therapy in Light of the Church's Witness

- **Ethical and Moral Implications**: Conversion therapy is fundamentally at odds with the ethical and moral teachings of Christianity. It promotes an agenda of change based on flawed premises and often results in emotional and psychological harm. Such practices undermine the ethical integrity of the Church and reflect poorly on its commitment to upholding Christian principles of love, dignity, and respect for all people.

- **Harmful Impact on Individuals**: The harmful impact of conversion therapy on individuals—

such as increased rates of depression, anxiety, and loss of self-esteem—contradicts the Church's mission to offer healing and support. By supporting or endorsing conversion therapy, the Church fails to provide the pastoral care and compassion that are central to its mission, thus harming those it seeks to serve and alienating them from the faith community.

- **Alienation of Marginalized Groups**: Conversion therapy can further alienate marginalized groups, particularly LGBTQ+ individuals, from the Church. This alienation can perpetuate a cycle of exclusion and mistrust, making it difficult for the Church to reach and minister to those who feel rejected or harmed by such practices. The witness of the Church is diminished when it fails to provide a welcoming and affirming environment for all people.

Strengthening the Church's Witness Through Affirmation and Support

- **Promoting Inclusivity and Respect**: To strengthen its witness, the Church should promote inclusivity and respect for all individuals. This involves rejecting harmful practices like conversion therapy and embracing approaches that affirm and support people in their authentic identities. By doing so, the Church aligns with its call to love and respect every person, reinforcing its positive witness in the world.

- **Providing Compassionate Care**: Offering compassionate and respectful care aligns with the Church's mission and enhances its credibility. This means focusing on supporting individuals through affirmation and understanding rather than seeking to change them. Compassionate care reflects the true spirit of Christian teaching and helps to rebuild trust with those who have been harmed by exclusionary practices.

- **Advocating for Ethical Practices**: The Church should advocate for ethical and evidence-based practices in mental health and pastoral care. By standing against conversion therapy and supporting practices that are grounded in respect and scientific validity, the Church can demonstrate its commitment to ethical principles and reinforce its positive witness.

Conclusion

Conversion therapy significantly harms the witness of the Church to the wider world by contradicting Christian values of love, compassion, and respect. Its association with harmful practices undermines the Church's credibility and misrepresents its core teachings. To uphold its witness and effectively communicate the gospel message, the Church must reject conversion therapy and embrace practices that affirm the dignity and worth of all individuals. By promoting inclusivity, providing compassionate care, and advocating for ethical practices, the Church can strengthen its witness and fulfill its mission to embody and share the love of Christ with the world.

28

Conversion therapy fundamentally fails to provide true pastoral support and care, highlighting its profound ethical and pastoral shortcomings. The essence of pastoral care is to offer compassion, guidance, and support that respects and nurtures individuals in their spiritual and emotional journeys. Conversion therapy, by attempting to alter fundamental aspects of an individual's identity, undermines these core principles and often exacerbates emotional and psychological distress.

The Core Principles of True Pastoral Support and Care

- **Compassion and Understanding**: True pastoral support is grounded in compassion and understanding. It involves empathizing with individuals' experiences, providing emotional and spiritual support, and helping them navigate their struggles with respect and sensitivity. This approach prioritizes the well-being and dignity of individuals, offering a safe and nurturing environment.

- **Respect for Identity**: Effective pastoral care respects and affirms individuals' identities as they are. It acknowledges the inherent worth and unique experiences of each person, supporting them in their journey of faith without seeking to change their core identity. This respect is crucial for building trust and fostering genuine relationships.

- **Encouragement and Healing**: Pastoral care aims to encourage and facilitate healing, offering support that aligns with the principles of love, acceptance, and understanding. It seeks to address emotional and spiritual needs in ways that promote well-being and personal growth, rather than imposing external standards or expectations.

The Wrongness of Conversion Therapy in Relation to Pastoral Care

- **Imposing Change Instead of Providing Support**: Conversion therapy fails to offer true pastoral care by focusing on changing an individual's sexual orientation or gender identity rather than providing support and understanding. This imposition of change contradicts the essence of pastoral care, which should be centered on supporting individuals in their authentic selves, not attempting to alter them.

- **Creating Emotional and Psychological Harm**: Rather than offering compassion, conversion therapy often creates significant emotional and psychological harm. It can lead to feelings of guilt, shame, and self-rejection, exacerbating distress rather than alleviating it. True pastoral care should seek to heal and uplift individuals, but conversion therapy typically results in emotional damage and worsened mental health outcomes.

- **Disregarding the Individual's Dignity**: By attempting to change fundamental aspects of a person's identity, conversion therapy disregards their inherent dignity and worth. True pastoral care involves affirming and valuing individuals as they are, recognizing their identity as a gift from God. Conversion therapy's failure to respect this dignity undermines its claim to be a form of pastoral support.

Providing True Pastoral Support in Contrast to Conversion Therapy

- **Affirmative and Supportive Approaches**: True pastoral support involves adopting affirmative and supportive approaches that respect individuals' identities. This means providing care that acknowledges and values who they are, offering encouragement and guidance in alignment with their authentic selves. Affirmative pastoral care fosters healing and growth without imposing unwanted changes.

- **Building Trust Through Respect**: Effective pastoral care builds trust by respecting individuals' experiences and identities. By avoiding harmful practices like conversion therapy and instead focusing on supportive, respectful engagement, pastoral care can create a safe and trusting environment. This trust is essential for effective support and meaningful spiritual growth.

- **Encouraging Authentic Growth**: True pastoral care encourages individuals to grow authentically in their faith and identity, rather than attempting to conform to external expectations. This involves helping individuals navigate their spiritual journeys in ways that affirm their true selves and support their overall well-being.

Conclusion

Conversion therapy fundamentally fails to provide true pastoral support and care by focusing on changing rather than affirming individuals' identities. Its approach contradicts the core principles of compassion, respect, and encouragement that define genuine pastoral care. By imposing harmful practices and disregarding the inherent dignity of individuals, conversion therapy undermines its claim to be a supportive practice. True pastoral support involves adopting affirmative and respectful approaches, building trust, and fostering authentic growth, all of which are incompatible with the goals and methods of conversion therapy.

29

Conversion therapy fundamentally disregards the belief that God's plans are higher than human understanding, revealing its profound ethical and theological flaws. In Christian doctrine, the understanding of God's will and divine purpose is considered far beyond human comprehension. Conversion therapy, by attempting to alter an individual's inherent identity based on limited human perspectives and assumptions, undermines this core belief in divine sovereignty and wisdom.

The Principle of Divine Sovereignty and Human Understanding

- **God's Sovereignty**: Christianity teaches that God is sovereign and His plans and purposes transcend human understanding (Isaiah 55:8-9). Believers trust that God's wisdom and intentions are perfect and beyond the scope of human insight. This principle underscores the belief that human attempts to modify or control aspects of a person's identity are presumptuous in the face of divine wisdom.

- **Respect for Divine Creation**: According to Christian faith, every person is created in the image of God

(Genesis 1:27). This divine creation is inherently good and reflects God's purpose. The belief in God's higher plans includes respecting and affirming the way individuals are created rather than attempting to alter them. This respect aligns with acknowledging that God's design and purpose for each person are beyond our limited understanding.

- **Submission to Divine Will**: Christians are called to submit to God's will and trust in His plans for their lives, understanding that His ways are higher than ours (Proverbs 3:5-6). This submission involves recognizing that God's design for each individual, including aspects related to identity and orientation, is part of His greater plan. Conversion therapy, by attempting to change these aspects, challenges this submission and disregards the trust in divine wisdom.

The Wrongness of Conversion Therapy in Light of Divine Sovereignty

- **Presumption Over Divine Wisdom**: Conversion therapy presumes to know better than God's design, attempting to change fundamental aspects of a person's identity based on limited human knowledge and understanding. This presumption is a direct challenge to the belief that God's plans and intentions are perfect and beyond human grasp. It reflects an inappropriate attempt to override or correct what is believed to be part of God's sovereign design.

- **Disrespect for Divine Creation**: By attempting to alter aspects of an individual's identity, conversion therapy disregards the belief that God's creation is inherently good and purposeful. It suggests that there is something flawed or in need of correction, contradicting the idea that every person's identity, as part of God's creation, is worthy of respect and affirmation. This disrespect challenges the theological understanding of divine creation and purpose.

- **Misalignment with Trust in God's Plan**: Conversion therapy is inconsistent with the Christian call to trust in God's plan and submit to His will. The therapy's focus on changing an individual's identity implies a lack of trust in God's design and purpose for that person. This misalignment with the principle of divine trust undermines the theological basis for accepting and affirming individuals as they are.

Affirming Divine Wisdom in Pastoral Care

- **Embracing Divine Design**: In pastoral care, acknowledging and embracing the belief that God's plans are higher than human understanding involves respecting and affirming individuals as they are. This approach aligns with the understanding that God's creation and purpose for each person are inherently good and worthy of acceptance.

- **Supporting Authentic Identity**: True pastoral care supports individuals in their authentic identities, trusting that God's design is perfect. By offering compassionate care that respects and affirms each person, the Church aligns with the belief in divine wisdom and demonstrates respect for God's creation.

- **Promoting Trust in Divine Purpose**: Pastoral support should encourage trust in God's purpose and design for each person. This involves guiding individuals in their spiritual journeys with the understanding that God's plans are beyond our comprehension and that His design for them is purposeful and good.

Conclusion

Conversion therapy fundamentally disregards the principle that God's plans and understanding are higher than human knowledge. By attempting to alter fundamental aspects of an individual's identity, conversion therapy presumes to know better than God's design and undermines trust in divine wisdom. True pastoral care should respect and affirm individuals as they are, embracing the belief that God's creation is inherently good and aligning with the understanding that

God's plans are perfect and beyond human comprehension. By rejecting conversion therapy and promoting support that honors divine design, the Church can uphold its commitment to respecting and affirming each person as part of God's sovereign plan.

30

Conversion therapy fundamentally invalidates individuals' personal experiences and testimonies, highlighting its profound ethical and emotional shortcomings. This practice disregards the lived experiences of those it seeks to "correct," treating their identities and personal narratives as problems to be fixed rather than aspects of their genuine selves. This invalidation contradicts core principles of respect, empathy, and understanding that are essential to both pastoral care and ethical treatment.

The Importance of Validating Personal Experiences

- **Respect for Individual Narratives**: Each person's experience and identity are shaped by a complex interplay of personal, cultural, and spiritual factors. Validating these experiences involves acknowledging and respecting individuals' narratives and perspectives as legitimate and significant. It recognizes that their lived experiences are integral to their identity and well-being.

- **Understanding and Empathy**: Genuine care and support require understanding and empathy toward individuals' experiences. This means listening to their stories, recognizing their struggles and triumphs, and offering support that aligns with their authentic selves. Validating personal experiences is a cornerstone of providing meaningful and compassionate care.

- **Affirmation of Identity**: Respecting personal experiences includes affirming individuals' identities as they are. This approach acknowledges that their identity is a valid expression of their self and their relationship with God, rather than something that needs to be changed or corrected.

The Wrongness of Conversion Therapy in Invalidating Personal Experiences

- **Dismissal of Authentic Identity**: Conversion therapy inherently dismisses the authenticity of individuals' personal experiences by implying that their identities are flawed and in need of change. This dismissal invalidates their lived experiences, disregarding their personal narratives and the significance of their self-understanding.

- **Imposition of External Standards**: By attempting to alter an individual's sexual orientation or gender identity, conversion therapy imposes external standards and norms, rather than respecting the individual's personal experiences and self-knowledge. This imposition contradicts the principle of respecting and valuing each person's unique journey and experiences.

- **Emotional and Psychological Harm**: The invalidation of personal experiences through conversion therapy can lead to significant emotional and psychological harm. Individuals subjected to this therapy may experience feelings of inadequacy, shame, and self-doubt when their genuine experiences and identities are deemed unacceptable or in need of change. This harm undermines their sense of self-worth and can lead to long-term psychological distress.

Promoting Respect and Validation in Pastoral Care

- **Affirming Personal Narratives**: True pastoral care involves affirming individuals' personal narratives and experiences. This means acknowledging and respecting their identities as integral to their self-understanding and relationship with God. By validating personal experiences, pastoral care can offer meaningful support and guidance that aligns with each individual's authentic self.

- **Offering Empathetic Support**: Providing empathetic support involves listening to and understanding individuals' experiences without judgment or attempts to alter their identities. This approach fosters a compassionate and supportive environment where individuals feel heard, valued, and respected.

- **Encouraging Authentic Self-Acceptance**: Pastoral care should encourage individuals to accept and embrace their authentic selves. By affirming their personal experiences and identities, pastoral support helps individuals build a healthy sense of self and navigate their spiritual and emotional journeys in a way that honors their true selves.

Conclusion

Conversion therapy fundamentally invalidates individuals' personal experiences and testimonies by treating their identities as problems to be fixed rather than authentic aspects of who they are. This invalidation contradicts core principles of respect, empathy, and understanding essential to ethical care and pastoral support. True pastoral care involves affirming personal narratives, offering empathetic support, and encouraging authentic self-acceptance. By rejecting conversion therapy and promoting respect for individuals' genuine experiences, the Church can provide meaningful and compassionate care that aligns with its core values and respects the dignity of each person.

31

Conversion therapy is fundamentally flawed because it contradicts the example set by Jesus, who did not force change upon people but instead offered acceptance, healing, and transformation through love and grace. Jesus' ministry was characterized by an invitation to change and growth through genuine relationship and understanding, rather than through coercion or attempts to alter individuals' fundamental identities.

The Example of Jesus in Relational Transformation

- **Invitation Rather than Coercion**: Jesus invited people to follow Him and experience transformation through relationship rather than coercion. For example, in the story of the rich young ruler (Matthew 19:16-22), Jesus invited the young man to sell his possessions and follow Him, but He did not force or coerce him. The invitation was personal and voluntary, respecting the young man's freedom to choose.

- **Healing and Acceptance**: Jesus' approach was centered on healing and acceptance. He interacted with those on the margins of society, such as tax collectors, sinners, and the sick, with compassion and grace. For instance, Jesus healed the woman with the issue of blood (Mark 5:25-34) not by demanding change but by offering her healing and restoration. His approach was one of empathy and respect for their inherent worth.

- **Respect for Individual Autonomy**: Jesus respected individuals' autonomy and did not impose change on them. He provided teachings and guidance but always allowed people to respond freely. His interactions were rooted in love and respect for individuals as they were, rather than an attempt to impose external standards or expectations.

The Wrongness of Conversion Therapy in Light of Jesus' Approach

- **Imposition of Change**: Conversion therapy is in direct contrast to Jesus' approach because it seeks to impose change upon individuals, attempting to alter their sexual orientation or gender identity based on external standards rather than respecting their inherent selves. This imposition reflects a disregard for the principles of relational transformation exemplified by Jesus.

- **Lack of Respect for Autonomy**: Conversion therapy often involves coercive methods and pressure, undermining individuals' autonomy and freedom. This is contrary to Jesus' example of respecting individuals' freedom to choose and respond to His invitation on their own terms. The therapy's disregard for personal autonomy contrasts sharply with Jesus' respectful and invitational approach.

- **Contradiction to Compassionate Care**: Jesus' ministry was characterized by compassionate care that acknowledged and affirmed individuals' inherent worth. Conversion therapy, by creating environments of shame and attempting to change core aspects of identity, fails to offer the compassionate care that Jesus modeled. It often leads to emotional and psychological harm rather than the healing and acceptance that Jesus provided.

Emulating Jesus' Approach in Pastoral Care

- **Offering Support and Understanding**: Pastoral care should emulate Jesus' approach by offering support and understanding rather than imposing change. This involves engaging with individuals in a way that respects their inherent identities and personal experiences, providing guidance and support that aligns with their authentic selves.

- **Respecting Personal Autonomy**: True pastoral care respects personal autonomy and freedom, allowing individuals to grow and explore their faith journey in ways that are authentic to them.

This approach aligns with Jesus' example of inviting rather than coercing, and respects individuals' freedom to make their own choices.

- **Providing Compassionate and Affirming Care**: In line with Jesus' ministry, pastoral care should be compassionate and affirming, focusing on the well-being of individuals and acknowledging their worth. This involves offering care that respects and supports individuals as they are, rather than seeking to change them according to external standards.

Conclusion

Conversion therapy fundamentally contradicts Jesus' example of not forcing change upon people. Jesus' approach was characterized by invitation, respect for autonomy, and compassionate care, rather than coercion or attempts to alter fundamental aspects of individuals' identities. Conversion therapy's imposition of change and disregard for personal autonomy and respect is at odds with the relational and respectful approach that Jesus modeled. To align with Jesus' example, pastoral care should focus on offering supportive, respectful, and compassionate care that affirms individuals as they are and respects their personal autonomy and inherent worth.

Conversion therapy fundamentally encourages people to live inauthentically, which starkly contrasts with the values of honesty, integrity, and authenticity central to Christian faith. By attempting to alter an individual's sexual orientation or gender identity, conversion therapy imposes external standards and expectations that compel individuals to deny their true selves, leading to a life of pretense rather than genuine self-expression.

The Principle of Authenticity in Christian Life

- **Call to Authentic Living**: Christianity emphasizes the importance of living authentically as a reflection of God's truth and love.

The Bible encourages believers to be true to themselves and to God, aligning their lives with their inner truth and divine calling (John 4:24, Philippians 4:8). Authenticity involves embracing who we are created to be and living in accordance with that truth.

- **Integrity of Self**: Living authentically means being honest with oneself and others about one's identity and experiences. Integrity requires that individuals align their outer actions with their inner reality, reflecting the truth of their identity in their everyday lives. This congruence is central to personal well-being and spiritual health.

- **Value of True Identity**: Christianity teaches that each person is created in the image of God (Genesis 1:27) and that God's creation is inherently good. Embracing one's true identity is seen as honoring God's design and purpose. Living authentically is a way to affirm and celebrate the value of being created in God's image.

The Wrongness of Conversion Therapy in Promoting Inauthenticity

- **Imposing False Standards**: Conversion therapy imposes external standards and expectations on individuals, often leading them to deny or suppress their true sexual orientation or gender identity. This imposition forces individuals to live according to standards that do not align with their authentic selves, encouraging a life of pretense rather than genuine self-expression.

- **Suppressing True Identity**: By attempting to change fundamental aspects of a person's identity, conversion therapy leads individuals to suppress their true selves. This suppression can result in emotional and psychological distress as individuals are pressured to conform to a false identity that does not reflect their true experiences or feelings.

- **Erosion of Self-Worth**: Encouraging inauthentic living through conversion therapy can erode individuals' sense of self-worth and self-esteem. When people are led to believe that their true identity is unacceptable or flawed, it undermines their confidence and acceptance of themselves, which can have long-lasting negative effects on their mental and emotional health.

Supporting Authentic Living in Pastoral Care

- **Affirming True Identity**: True pastoral care involves affirming individuals' true identities and supporting them in living authentically. This means recognizing and valuing who they are, rather than imposing external standards or expectations. Affirmative pastoral care respects and celebrates individuals' genuine selves as part of God's creation.

- **Encouraging Honest Expression**: Pastoral support should encourage honest expression and self-discovery, helping individuals align their outer lives with their inner truth. This approach supports personal well-being and spiritual health by allowing people to live in accordance with their authentic identities.

- **Providing Compassionate and Respectful Care**: Offering compassionate and respectful care involves accepting individuals as they are and supporting them in their journey of self-acceptance and authenticity. This aligns with Christian principles of love and respect, fostering an environment where individuals can thrive without being pressured to conform to an inauthentic identity.

Conclusion

Conversion therapy fundamentally encourages individuals to live inauthentically by imposing external standards and expectations that compel them to deny their true identities. This approach is contrary to the Christian values of authenticity, integrity, and respect for God's creation. True pastoral care should focus on affirming individuals' genuine selves, supporting them in living authentically, and providing compassionate care that respects and celebrates their true identities. By rejecting conversion therapy and promoting authentic living, the Church can uphold its commitment to honoring the dignity and worth of every person as created in the image of God.

33

Conversion therapy fundamentally oversimplifies the complex issues of sin and human sexuality, revealing its deep theological and ethical flaws. By attempting to address and "correct" what it perceives as deviations from normative standards, conversion therapy reduces the intricate and nuanced realities of human sexuality to simplistic and often harmful frameworks. This oversimplification disregards the rich and complex understanding of human identity and sin found in Christian theology.

The Complexity of Sin and Human Sexuality

- **Nuanced Understanding of Sin**: In Christian theology, sin is understood as a multifaceted issue that encompasses more than mere actions or behaviors; it involves the condition of the heart and the human relationship with God. Sin is not merely about isolated acts but about a broader disalignment with divine will and the need for reconciliation and transformation through grace.

- **Diverse Expressions of Human Sexuality**: Human sexuality is a complex aspect of human identity that includes emotional, relational, and biological dimensions. It cannot be reduced to a single dimension or simplified into binary categories. Christian theology recognizes the diversity of human experiences and the importance of understanding sexuality within a holistic context.

- **Holistic View of Identity**: Christian teaching emphasizes that every person is created in the image of God (Genesis 1:27) and that each individual's identity is multifaceted and deeply rooted in divine creation. This holistic view encompasses all aspects of human life, including sexuality, and recognizes the importance of respecting and understanding each person's unique experiences and struggles.

The Wrongness of Conversion Therapy in Oversimplifying These Issues

- **Reductionist Approach**: Conversion therapy adopts a reductionist approach by attempting to "fix" or "correct" sexual orientation or gender identity based on oversimplified beliefs about sin and sexuality. This approach fails to acknowledge the complex interplay of biological, psychological, and spiritual factors that contribute to a person's sexual orientation or gender identity.

- **Misinterpretation of Scriptural Teachings**: Conversion therapy often misinterprets or selectively uses scriptural teachings to support its agenda, ignoring the broader and more nuanced theological understanding of sin and human sexuality. By focusing on specific texts or interpretations, it oversimplifies the rich and diverse biblical perspectives on human identity and relationships.

- **Neglect of Individual Complexity**: The therapy disregards the individual complexity of human sexuality and the personal experiences that shape it. It imposes a one-size-fits-all solution that fails to take into account the unique and varied experiences of individuals, leading to harmful and ineffective outcomes.

Embracing a More Nuanced Understanding in Pastoral Care

- **Recognizing Diversity and Complexity**: True pastoral care involves recognizing and respecting the diversity and complexity of human sexuality. This means understanding that sexuality is a deeply personal and multifaceted aspect of identity that cannot be reduced to simplistic categories or solutions.

- **Providing Holistic Support**: Pastoral care should provide holistic support that addresses the full spectrum of human experience, including the emotional, relational, and spiritual aspects of sexuality. This involves offering guidance and support that respects and affirms individuals' experiences rather than attempting to impose external standards.

- **Promoting Understanding and Compassion**: By embracing a nuanced understanding of sin and human sexuality, pastoral care can offer compassion and understanding that align with Christian values of love and grace. This approach respects individuals' unique experiences and provides support that is grounded in empathy and respect for their authentic selves.

Conclusion

Conversion therapy fundamentally oversimplifies the complex issues of sin and human sexuality by reducing them to simplistic frameworks and attempting to impose uniform solutions. This reductionist approach disregards the rich and nuanced understanding of human identity found in Christian theology. True pastoral care should embrace the complexity and diversity of human sexuality, providing support that respects and affirms individuals' unique experiences. By rejecting the oversimplified and harmful approaches of conversion therapy, the Church can offer compassionate and holistic care that aligns with a more profound and respectful understanding of sin and human sexuality.

34

Conversion therapy fails to seek justice and mercy as commanded by God, highlighting its fundamental ethical and theological shortcomings. The Bible consistently emphasizes the importance of justice and mercy as central aspects of God's character and His expectations for humanity. By focusing on attempts to alter individuals' sexual orientation or gender identity, conversion therapy neglects these divine imperatives and often leads to harm rather than healing.

The Biblical Call for Justice and Mercy

- **Justice and Mercy as Divine Commands**: Throughout Scripture, God commands His people to act justly and to love mercy. Micah 6:8 summarizes this command succinctly: "He has shown you, O mortal, what is good. And what does the Lord require of you? To act justly and to love mercy and to walk humbly with your God." These principles are foundational to understanding God's will and reflect His character.

- **Justice as Fairness and Equity**: Biblical justice involves treating people with fairness and equity, ensuring that all individuals are treated with dignity and respect. It is about upholding the rights of the vulnerable and marginalized, advocating for their well-being, and addressing injustices in a manner consistent with God's love and righteousness.

- **Mercy as Compassion and Understanding**: Mercy is characterized by compassion, forgiveness, and understanding. Jesus' teachings and actions consistently emphasize mercy, urging believers to show kindness and empathy toward others, especially those who are suffering or marginalized. For instance, in Matthew 5:7, Jesus states, "Blessed are the merciful, for they will be shown mercy."

The Wrongness of Conversion Therapy in Light of Justice and Mercy

- **Injustice Through Coercion and Harm**: Conversion therapy often involves coercive practices and can lead to significant psychological and emotional harm. By imposing external standards and attempting to change fundamental aspects of an individual's identity, it fails to treat people with the fairness and respect that justice demands. This coercion contradicts the principle of justice, which requires treating individuals with dignity and ensuring their well-being.

- **Lack of Compassion and Understanding**: Conversion therapy often disregards the principle of mercy by failing to offer compassion and understanding. Instead of approaching individuals with empathy and support, it frequently imposes judgment and attempts to alter their identities based on misguided interpretations of Scripture. This approach is inconsistent with the call to love mercy and to act with kindness toward others.

- **Neglecting the Well-being of Individuals**: By prioritizing attempts to change individuals rather than supporting their authentic selves, conversion therapy neglects their emotional and psychological well-being. True justice and mercy involve prioritizing the health and dignity of individuals, providing care that aligns with their true identity and supports their overall well-being.

Promoting Justice and Mercy in Pastoral Care

- **Affirming Dignity and Worth**: True pastoral care seeks to affirm the dignity and worth of every individual, aligning with the biblical call for justice. This means respecting and valuing individuals as they are, without attempting to impose changes that disregard their inherent identity.

- **Offering Compassionate Support**: Pastoral care should

embody mercy by offering compassionate and understanding support. This involves listening to individuals' experiences, providing emotional and spiritual support that aligns with their true selves, and showing empathy and kindness in all interactions.

- **Advocating for Well-being and Respect**: In line with justice and mercy, pastoral care should advocate for the well-being and respect of all individuals. This includes addressing harmful practices like conversion therapy and promoting approaches that support and affirm individuals' identities, ensuring that their rights and dignity are upheld.

Conclusion

Conversion therapy fails to seek justice and mercy as commanded by God by engaging in practices that are coercive, harmful, and lacking in compassion. This approach contradicts the biblical principles of fairness, respect, and empathy that are central to God's commands. True pastoral care should reflect the divine call for justice and mercy by affirming individuals' dignity, offering compassionate support, and advocating for their well-being. By rejecting conversion therapy and embracing practices that honor these principles, the Church can align with God's commands and offer care that is truly just and merciful.

35

Conversion therapy reflects cultural prejudices rather than biblical truths, exposing its inherent flaws and ethical issues. By prioritizing societal biases and norms over the fundamental principles of Christian teaching, conversion therapy distorts the message of the Gospel and undermines the core values of compassion, acceptance, and respect for all individuals.

The Distinction Between Cultural Prejudices and Biblical Truths

- **Cultural Prejudices**: Cultural prejudices are biases and stereotypes that arise from societal norms, traditions, and misunderstandings.

These prejudices often reflect the dominant attitudes of a particular time and place, which can be influenced by various social, political, and historical factors. When these prejudices are imposed on individuals, they can lead to harmful practices and discrimination.

- **Biblical Truths**: Biblical truths are the teachings and principles found in Scripture that reflect God's character and His will for humanity. These truths emphasize love, acceptance, and the inherent worth of every person created in God's image. They call for treating others with dignity and respect, regardless of societal biases or cultural norms.

The Wrongness of Conversion Therapy in Reflecting Cultural Prejudices

- **Imposition of Societal Norms**: Conversion therapy often stems from cultural prejudices that view non-heteronormative identities as deviant or undesirable. These societal norms are then imposed on individuals, attempting to change their sexual orientation or gender identity to fit within a narrow and prejudiced framework. This imposition reflects cultural biases rather than the inclusive and affirming message of the Gospel.

- **Misinterpretation of Scripture**: Conversion therapy frequently relies on selective or misinterpreted readings of Scripture to support its practices. These interpretations often reflect the cultural prejudices of the time rather than the broader, more nuanced teachings of the Bible. For example, texts that are used to condemn LGBTQ+ identities are often taken out of context and do not reflect the full message of love, grace, and inclusion found in Jesus' teachings.

- **Disregard for Inherent Dignity**: By attempting to alter fundamental aspects of an individual's identity, conversion therapy disregards the inherent dignity and worth of every person as created in God's image. This disregard is a manifestation of cultural prejudices that fail to recognize the biblical truth of each person's value and the importance of affirming their true selves.

Embracing Biblical Truths in Pastoral Care

- **Affirmation of Inherent Worth**: True pastoral care should reflect the biblical truth that every person is created in the image of God and is worthy of respect and love (Genesis 1:27). This involves affirming individuals' identities and treating them with dignity, rather than imposing cultural prejudices or attempting to change who they are.

- **Reflecting Jesus' Teachings**: Jesus' ministry was characterized by acceptance and love for all people, including those marginalized by society (Matthew 9:10-13, Luke 7:36-50). Pastoral care should mirror this aspect of Jesus' teaching by providing support that is inclusive and affirming, aligning with the true message of the Gospel.

- **Challenging Cultural Biases**: In offering pastoral care, it is essential to challenge and reject cultural biases that conflict with biblical truths. This means advocating for practices and attitudes that align with the inclusive and compassionate teachings of Scripture, rather than conforming to societal prejudices.

Conclusion

Conversion therapy reflects cultural prejudices rather than biblical truths by imposing societal norms and biases on individuals, rather than upholding the principles of love, acceptance, and respect found in Scripture. It distorts the message of the Gospel and undermines the core Christian values of inherent dignity and worth. True pastoral care should embrace biblical truths by affirming individuals' identities, reflecting Jesus' inclusive teachings, and challenging cultural biases that conflict with the message of love and acceptance in the Bible. By rejecting conversion therapy and promoting a compassionate, biblically grounded approach, the Church can more faithfully embody the true message of the Gospel.

36

Conversion therapy drives people away from a relationship with God by fostering an environment of shame, alienation, and emotional distress. Instead of drawing individuals closer to God, this practice often results in significant harm to their spiritual and emotional well-being, leading to a rupture in their connection with the divine and the faith community. The approach and methods of conversion therapy are fundamentally at odds with the nature of God's love and the principles of spiritual nurturing and support.

The Impact of Conversion Therapy on Spiritual Well-Being

- **Fostering Shame and Guilt**: Conversion therapy often instills deep feelings of shame and guilt in individuals by implying that their sexual orientation or gender identity is inherently flawed or sinful. This creates an environment where individuals feel rejected by both their faith community and by God, undermining their sense of worth and their ability to experience God's unconditional love.

- **Creating Emotional Distress**: The coercive techniques used in conversion therapy can lead to significant emotional and psychological distress. The stress of trying to conform to imposed norms, combined with the rejection of one's true self, can lead to anxiety, depression, and other mental health issues. This distress can make it difficult for individuals to experience spiritual comfort and connection.

- **Alienation from the Faith Community**: Conversion therapy can result in individuals feeling alienated from their faith community. The process often involves isolating individuals from supportive relationships and reinforcing a sense of being an outsider or unworthy. This alienation can further erode their connection to the community and to God, as they may feel rejected by both.

The Wrongness of Conversion Therapy in Light of Spiritual Relationship

- **Contradiction to God's Unconditional Love**: God's love is described in Scripture as unconditional and inclusive (John 3:16, Romans 5:8). Conversion therapy, by contrast, operates on the premise that certain aspects of a person's identity are unacceptable. This approach contradicts the core message of God's love, which affirms individuals as they are rather than attempting to change them.

- **Misalignment with the Gospel's Message**: The Gospel message is one of acceptance, grace, and healing (Matthew 11:28-30, 2 Corinthians

5:18). Conversion therapy, however, often emphasizes judgment and the need for change, which misaligns with the Gospel's call to embrace people with compassion and support them in their spiritual journey.

- **Undermining Spiritual Growth**: Genuine spiritual growth comes from a place of acceptance and understanding, where individuals feel safe to explore and deepen their relationship with God. Conversion therapy's emphasis on changing one's fundamental identity rather than supporting authentic self-discovery undermines this growth, leading individuals to distance themselves from their faith.

Encouraging a Positive Spiritual Relationship

- **Embracing Unconditional Acceptance**: True pastoral care should embrace the unconditional acceptance and love that God offers. This involves creating a supportive environment where individuals feel valued and accepted, regardless of their sexual orientation or gender identity. By reflecting God's inclusive love, pastoral care can help individuals build a closer relationship with God.

- **Providing Supportive Relationships**: Encouraging spiritual growth involves fostering supportive relationships within the faith community. This means offering empathy, understanding, and encouragement, rather than imposing change or judgment. Such relationships help individuals feel connected and supported in their spiritual journey.

- **Affirming Authentic Identities**: Pastoral care should affirm individuals' authentic identities as part of their relationship with God. This approach respects and honors their true selves, allowing them to grow spiritually in a manner that aligns with their authentic identity and experiences.

Conclusion

Conversion therapy drives people away from a relationship with God by fostering shame, emotional distress, and alienation, which are fundamentally at odds with the principles of divine love and support found in Scripture. It contradicts the unconditional acceptance and grace that characterize God's relationship with humanity. True pastoral care should focus on embracing God's love, providing supportive relationships, and affirming individuals' authentic identities. By rejecting conversion therapy and promoting an inclusive and compassionate approach, the Church can help individuals develop a meaningful and supportive relationship with God.

37

Conversion therapy fundamentally contradicts the principle of "Do unto others as you would have them do unto you," also known as the Golden Rule, which is a cornerstone of ethical behavior and Christian teaching. This principle, as articulated in Matthew 7:12 ("So in everything, do to others what you would have them do to you, for this sums up the Law and the Prophets"), emphasizes treating others with the same respect, kindness, and empathy that one would wish for oneself. Conversion therapy, however, fails to align with this principle by imposing harmful practices on individuals in ways that violate their inherent dignity and well-being.

The Golden Rule in Christian Teaching

- **Principle of Reciprocity**: The Golden Rule teaches the importance of reciprocity in our interactions with others. It encourages individuals to consider how their actions affect others and to act with empathy and respect. This principle underlines the idea that ethical behavior involves treating others with the same consideration and compassion that one would desire for oneself.

- **Foundation of Ethical Behavior**: Jesus taught the Golden Rule as a summary of the ethical teachings found in the Law and the Prophets. It serves as a guide for moral conduct, emphasizing that how we treat others should be guided by our own desire for fairness and kindness.

- **Call to Compassion and Respect**: The Golden Rule is a call to compassion and respect, urging individuals to act in ways that affirm and uphold the dignity and worth of others. It requires looking beyond personal biases and considering the impact of one's actions on others.

The Wrongness of Conversion Therapy in Relation to the Golden Rule

- **Imposing Harmful Practices**: Conversion therapy imposes practices that attempt to change an individual's sexual orientation or gender identity, often through methods that can cause significant psychological and emotional harm. This imposition disregards the principle of treating others with the respect and empathy one would wish for oneself. If those advocating for conversion therapy were in the position of those undergoing such treatments, they would likely not wish to endure the emotional and psychological suffering associated with these practices.

- **Ignoring Inherent Dignity**: The principle of "Do unto others" involves recognizing and respecting the inherent dignity of each person. Conversion therapy undermines this dignity by attempting to alter fundamental aspects of an individual's identity, thereby failing to honor their true selves. Respecting others means affirming their identities and supporting their well-being, not attempting to change or suppress them based on external standards.

- **Creating Emotional and Psychological Distress**: Conversion therapy often leads to emotional and psychological distress, including feelings of shame, guilt, and self-rejection. This outcome is contrary to the Golden Rule, which calls for actions that promote the well-being and happiness of others. Subjecting individuals to practices that result in harm and distress fails to meet the standard of empathy and respect that the Golden Rule demands.

Aligning with the Golden Rule in Pastoral Care

- **Offering Compassionate Support**: True pastoral care should embody the Golden Rule by providing compassionate and supportive care. This involves treating individuals with kindness, understanding, and empathy, and respecting their authentic identities. Such care reflects the desire to be treated with dignity and respect.

- **Affirming Authentic Identity**: Pastoral care should affirm individuals' true identities and support their well-being. This approach aligns with the Golden Rule by respecting each person's unique identity and experiences, rather than imposing changes that disregard their inherent worth.

- **Promoting Emotional Well-being**: By focusing on the emotional and psychological well-being of individuals, pastoral care can ensure that actions and support align with the principle of treating others as one would wish to be treated. This includes offering care that uplifts and nurtures rather than harms.

Conclusion

Conversion therapy fundamentally violates the principle of "Do unto others as you would have them do unto you" by imposing harmful practices that disrespect and undermine the dignity of individuals. The Golden Rule calls for empathy, respect, and compassion in our interactions, emphasizing that we should treat others with the same kindness and consideration that we would desire for ourselves. Conversion therapy fails to meet this standard by causing harm and distress, rather than offering the respect and support that the Golden Rule demands. True pastoral care should align with this principle by affirming individuals' authentic identities, offering compassionate support, and promoting their well-being. By rejecting conversion therapy and embracing practices that honor the Golden Rule, the Church can better reflect the values of love and respect central to Christian teaching.

38

Conversion therapy fundamentally misunderstands the nature of repentance, a key concept in Christian faith and practice. The process of repentance, as described in Scripture, involves a heartfelt turning away from sin and a genuine transformation of the heart and mind in response to God's grace. Conversion therapy, however, misconstrues this spiritual process by attempting to alter a person's sexual orientation or gender identity through coercive or manipulative means, rather than fostering authentic spiritual growth and transformation.

The Biblical Understanding of Repentance

- **Heartfelt Transformation**: True repentance in the Christian faith involves a deep, personal transformation that comes from a sincere change of heart and mind. This transformation is driven by a response to God's grace and forgiveness, leading to a reorientation of one's life in alignment with God's will (Acts 3:19, 2 Corinthians 7:10).

- **Response to God's Grace**: Biblical repentance is not merely about changing behaviors but about a profound response to God's grace. It reflects an understanding of one's need for divine mercy and a desire to live in a way that honors God's love and righteousness (Ezekiel 36:26, Luke 15:7).

- **Inner Change Over External Conformity**: Genuine repentance involves inner change rather than external conformity. It's about the renewal of the inner self, where one's desires and attitudes are aligned with God's will, rather than merely adhering to external standards or pressures.

The Wrongness of Conversion Therapy in Relation to Repentance

- **Misapplication of Repentance**: Conversion therapy misapplies the concept of repentance by treating it as a means to change fundamental aspects of a person's identity, such as their sexual orientation or gender identity. Instead of focusing on a genuine transformation of the heart and mind, it seeks to impose external changes based on societal or religious norms, which is inconsistent with the biblical understanding of repentance.

- **Coercive Methods**: Conversion therapy often employs coercive methods that aim to force individuals to conform to certain norms rather than facilitating a voluntary and heartfelt transformation. This approach disregards the role of genuine repentance, which is a voluntary response to God's grace and involves an authentic change of heart, not a forced external adjustment (Matthew 23:27-28).

- **Ignoring Authentic Spiritual Growth**: By focusing on changing an individual's sexual orientation or gender identity, conversion therapy overlooks the deeper aspects of spiritual growth and repentance. It fails to address the root causes of spiritual and emotional struggles, instead imposing superficial changes that do not align with the true nature of repentance as an inward transformation.

Aligning Pastoral Care with True Repentance

- **Fostering Genuine Transformation**: True pastoral care should focus on fostering genuine spiritual transformation through a heartfelt response to God's grace. This involves encouraging individuals to explore their faith deeply, seek personal growth, and align their lives with God's will from an authentic and voluntary perspective.

- **Supporting Authentic Identity**: Pastoral care should respect and support individuals' authentic identities, allowing them to experience spiritual growth in a manner that aligns with their true selves. This approach recognizes that repentance and transformation are about internal change and relationship with God, rather than external conformity to imposed standards.

- **Encouraging Voluntary Change**: Encouraging repentance involves guiding individuals towards a voluntary and heartfelt response to God's love and forgiveness. Pastoral care should avoid coercive practices and instead provide support that helps individuals grow spiritually in a way that is true to their personal experiences and identity.

Conclusion

Conversion therapy fundamentally misunderstands the nature of repentance by attempting to impose external changes rather than fostering a genuine, heartfelt transformation of the heart and mind. True repentance, as described in Scripture, involves an inner change in response to God's grace, rather than superficial or coercive alterations of one's identity. Conversion therapy's focus on changing individuals' sexual orientation or gender identity through external means contradicts the biblical understanding of repentance. True pastoral care should align with this understanding by supporting genuine spiritual growth, respecting authentic identities, and encouraging voluntary and heartfelt transformation. By rejecting conversion therapy and embracing practices that reflect the true nature of repentance, the Church can offer more meaningful and compassionate support to individuals seeking to grow in their faith.

39

Conversion therapy fundamentally neglects the concept of grace, which is central to Christianity and vital to understanding the relationship between God and humanity. Grace, as described in Christian doctrine, is the unearned, unconditional love and favor of God extended to all people, regardless of their actions or identity. It is a core element of the Gospel and the foundation of Christian faith. Conversion therapy's practices, however, undermine this central tenet by prioritizing attempts to change individuals rather than embracing them with the unconditional love and acceptance that grace embodies.

The Centrality of Grace in Christianity

- **Unconditional Love**: Grace represents God's unconditional love for all people, extending forgiveness and acceptance regardless of their past actions or inherent characteristics (Ephesians 2:8-9, Romans 5:8). It is a demonstration of God's commitment to humanity's well-being, independent of their ability to meet certain standards or norms.

- **Acceptance of Imperfection**: The concept of grace acknowledges human imperfection and provides a pathway for reconciliation and transformation through God's love. It emphasizes that individuals are accepted and valued by God as they are, without needing to conform to specific external expectations (2 Corinthians 12:9, Titus 3:5).

- **Transformation Through Love**: Grace is transformative, not by forcing changes, but by inspiring a genuine response to God's love. It enables individuals to grow and change from a place of acceptance and love, rather than fear or condemnation (John 3:16, 1 John 4:10).

The Wrongness of Conversion Therapy in Relation to Grace

- **Undermines Unconditional Love**: Conversion therapy contradicts the concept of grace by implying that certain aspects of an individual's identity are unacceptable and must be changed. This approach undermines the notion of unconditional love by suggesting that individuals must alter their inherent characteristics to be worthy of acceptance and support.

- **Promotes Conditional Acceptance**: The practices of conversion therapy promote conditional acceptance, where individuals are only valued if they conform to certain standards or norms. This approach is contrary to the grace that God offers, which is unconditional and not based on meeting specific criteria (Romans 8:38-39, Galatians 2:21).

- **Fails to Reflect Transformative Love**: Conversion therapy's methods often involve coercion and attempts to force change, rather than fostering an environment where transformation can occur through the genuine and transformative power of God's love. This approach does not reflect the biblical understanding of grace, which transforms lives through acceptance and love rather than through external pressures (Ephesians 4:32, Colossians 3:13).

Embracing Grace in Pastoral Care

- **Affirming Unconditional Acceptance**: Pastoral care should reflect the unconditional acceptance that grace embodies. This means affirming individuals' inherent worth and supporting them in their journey without imposing conditions or attempting to change their fundamental identity.

- **Offering Compassion and Forgiveness**: True pastoral care involves offering compassion and forgiveness in the spirit of grace. It means providing support and understanding that is rooted in love and acceptance, rather than judgment or condemnation.

- **Supporting Genuine Growth**: Grace enables genuine spiritual growth by fostering a nurturing and accepting environment. Pastoral care should support individuals in their spiritual journey by focusing on love and acceptance, allowing growth and transformation to occur naturally through their relationship with God.

Conclusion

Conversion therapy neglects the concept of grace central to Christianity by imposing conditions and attempting to change individuals' inherent identities, rather than embracing them with unconditional love and acceptance. Grace, as the unearned favor of God, emphasizes acceptance, compassion, and the transformative power of love. Conversion therapy's focus on altering individuals rather than affirming their worth and supporting their growth from a place of acceptance contradicts the fundamental principles of grace. True pastoral care should align with the concept of grace by offering unconditional acceptance, compassion, and support, thereby reflecting the genuine love and forgiveness that God extends to all people.

40

Conversion therapy obstructs individuals' spiritual growth and maturity by prioritizing external changes over internal transformation, fostering an environment of fear and shame rather than one of genuine spiritual development. Spiritual growth in Christianity involves deepening one's relationship with God, understanding His will, and becoming more aligned with His love and grace. Conversion therapy disrupts this process by imposing superficial changes and creating obstacles that hinder true spiritual maturity.

Spiritual Growth and Maturity in Christianity

- **Deepening Relationship with God**: Spiritual growth involves developing a deeper, more authentic relationship with God, characterized by trust, understanding, and love. This relationship is nurtured through prayer, reflection, and personal experiences of God's grace and guidance (James 4:8, Philippians 3:10).

- **Understanding and Alignment with God's Will**: Growing spiritually means seeking to understand and align one's life with God's will. This involves personal reflection, learning from Scripture, and responding to God's call in a way that reflects His love and righteousness (Romans 12:2, Colossians 1:10).

- **Authentic Transformation**: True spiritual maturity involves a transformation that comes from within, driven by a heartfelt response to God's love and grace. This transformation is an ongoing process of becoming more like Christ in one's character and actions (2 Corinthians 5:17, Galatians 5:22-23).

The Wrongness of Conversion Therapy in Relation to Spiritual Growth

- **Imposing External Changes**: Conversion therapy focuses on altering an individual's sexual orientation or gender identity through external methods, rather than fostering internal spiritual growth. This approach prioritizes superficial compliance with specific norms over the deep, authentic transformation that true spiritual growth requires.

- **Creating Obstacles to Authentic Self-Understanding**: By attempting to change fundamental aspects of a person's identity, conversion therapy can create significant internal conflict and self-doubt. This conflict obstructs individuals from fully understanding and accepting themselves as part of their spiritual journey, hindering their ability to grow and mature spiritually (Psalm 139:14, Ephesians 2:10).

- **Fostering Fear and Shame**: Conversion therapy often relies on fear and shame as motivational tools, which are counterproductive to spiritual growth. These emotions can lead to feelings of worthlessness and alienation, which obstruct individuals' ability to experience God's love and grace fully and to grow spiritually in a healthy and supportive environment (1 John 4:18, Romans 8:1).

Encouraging Genuine Spiritual Growth in Pastoral Care

- **Promoting Acceptance and Love**: True pastoral care should focus on promoting acceptance and love, reflecting God's unconditional grace. By creating a nurturing environment where individuals are valued as they are, pastoral care supports authentic spiritual growth and helps individuals develop a deeper relationship with God.

- **Supporting Authentic Self-Understanding**: Pastoral care should encourage individuals to explore and understand their authentic selves as part of their spiritual journey. This involves affirming their inherent worth and supporting their growth in a manner that aligns with their true identity and experiences (Jeremiah 29:11, Proverbs 3:5-6).

- **Encouraging a Healthy Relationship with God**: A supportive pastoral approach should foster a healthy and positive relationship with God, free from fear and shame. This involves guiding individuals in their spiritual practices and helping them experience God's love and grace in a way that facilitates genuine growth and maturity (Matthew 11:28-30, 2 Timothy 1:7).

Conclusion

Conversion therapy obstructs individuals' spiritual growth and maturity by prioritizing external changes and creating barriers to authentic self-understanding and transformation. True spiritual growth involves a deepening relationship with God, understanding His will, and experiencing genuine internal transformation through His grace. Conversion therapy's focus on altering fundamental aspects of identity and its reliance on fear and shame hinder this process, preventing individuals from fully engaging in their spiritual journey. True pastoral care should support spiritual growth by fostering acceptance, promoting authentic self-understanding, and encouraging a healthy relationship with God. By rejecting conversion therapy and embracing practices that align with genuine spiritual development, the Church can better support individuals in their journey towards spiritual maturity.

41

Conversion therapy is fundamentally at odds with the example set by Jesus, who healed with compassion and never used coercion. Jesus' ministry was characterized by acts of love, understanding, and gentle guidance, not by forceful attempts to change or control individuals. Conversion therapy, however, employs methods that are coercive and often harmful, deviating from the compassionate and respectful approach exemplified by Jesus.

Jesus' Healing Ministry

- **Compassionate Approach**: Jesus healed people out of genuine compassion, responding to their needs with empathy and kindness. His healing was a manifestation of His love and care, aimed at restoring wholeness and well-being in a manner that respected each person's dignity and humanity (Matthew 14:14, Mark 1:41).

- **Respectful of Personal Dignity**: Jesus respected the personal dignity and autonomy of those He healed. He did not impose His will upon them but offered healing and restoration in a way that honored their individual experiences and choices (Luke 8:43-48, John 4:7-10).

- **Inviting Transformation**: Jesus invited people to follow Him and embrace transformation through love and acceptance. He did not use coercion or force but extended an open invitation for those who were willing to respond to His message of grace and forgiveness (Matthew 11:28-30, John 15:9-17).

The Wrongness of Conversion Therapy in Relation to Jesus' Approach

- **Coercive Methods**: Conversion therapy often relies on coercive techniques to attempt to change individuals' sexual orientation or gender identity. This approach contradicts Jesus' method of healing, which was based on compassion and voluntary response rather than manipulation and pressure. Coercion in conversion therapy disregards the individual's autonomy and personal dignity, which were central to Jesus' interactions (Matthew 7:12, Galatians 5:13).

- **Creating Harm Rather Than Healing**: Instead of bringing healing and restoration, conversion therapy can cause significant psychological and emotional harm. This harm is contrary to Jesus' example, who brought healing that led to wholeness and peace. The adverse effects of conversion therapy, such as increased feelings of shame and self-rejection, are inconsistent with the compassionate and restorative nature of Jesus' ministry (John 10:10, 1 John 4:18).

- **Disrespecting Personal Identity**: Conversion therapy often fails to respect the personal identity and experiences of individuals, imposing external standards and expectations that undermine their inherent worth. Jesus, by contrast, engaged with individuals in a manner that respected their personal experiences and identities, offering healing and acceptance without demanding change (Luke 19:5-10, John 8:1-11).

Aligning Pastoral Care with Jesus' Compassionate Example

- **Practicing Compassion**: Pastoral care should mirror Jesus' compassionate approach by offering support, understanding, and empathy. This involves engaging with individuals in a way that respects their experiences and identities, rather than imposing external changes or using coercive methods (Colossians 3:12-14, Philippians 2:1-4).

- **Supporting Authentic Healing**: True pastoral care aims to support authentic healing and growth through love and acceptance. It should create a nurturing environment where individuals can explore their faith and well-being without fear or shame, aligning with the restorative nature of Jesus' ministry (James 5:14-16, 2 Corinthians 1:3-4).

- **Respecting Personal Dignity**: Pastoral care should honor the personal dignity and autonomy of each individual, providing support that aligns with their authentic selves and experiences. This approach reflects the respect and care that Jesus demonstrated in His healing ministry (Romans 12:10, 1 Peter 3:8-9).

Conclusion

Conversion therapy is fundamentally at odds with Jesus' approach to healing, which was characterized by compassion, respect, and voluntary response rather than coercion and manipulation. Jesus' ministry was marked by a healing that restored wholeness and dignity through love and empathy, not through forceful attempts to change individuals. Conversion therapy's reliance on coercive methods and its potential for causing harm contradict the compassionate and respectful example set by Jesus. True pastoral care should reflect Jesus' example by offering support and healing through compassion, respecting personal dignity, and fostering authentic growth and well-being. By rejecting conversion therapy and embracing a more compassionate and respectful approach, the Church can better align with the values of love and care exemplified by Jesus.

42

Conversion therapy provides false teaching contrary to the Gospel by distorting the core message of Christianity, which centers on unconditional love, grace, and acceptance. The Gospel, as revealed in the life and teachings of Jesus Christ, emphasizes the inherent worth of every individual and the transformative power of God's love. Conversion therapy, however, promotes a harmful narrative that conflicts with these central tenets by suggesting that fundamental aspects of a person's identity are inherently wrong and need to be changed through coercive means.

The Gospel Message

- **Unconditional Love and Grace**: The Gospel proclaims God's unconditional love for all people and His offer of grace regardless of their past actions or personal characteristics (John 3:16, Ephesians 2:8-9). This message emphasizes that every person is valued and accepted by God as they are, and that transformation comes through God's grace, not through human efforts to conform to external standards.

- **Inherent Worth of Every Individual**: The teachings of Jesus affirm the inherent worth and dignity of every individual. Jesus' interactions with people were characterized by acceptance and respect, acknowledging their value and offering healing and forgiveness (Luke 15:1-7, John 4:7-26).

- **Transformation through Love**: The Gospel teaches that transformation occurs through a response to God's love and grace, not through coercion or force. Genuine spiritual growth involves an inner transformation driven by a deepening relationship with God and a response to His love (2 Corinthians 5:17, Romans 12:2).

The Wrongness of Conversion Therapy in Relation to the Gospel

- **Contradicts Unconditional Love**: Conversion therapy contradicts the Gospel's message of unconditional love by suggesting that certain aspects of a person's identity are unacceptable and must be changed. This view undermines the core principle that God's love is unconditional and that individuals are accepted and valued as they are (Romans 5:8, 1 John 4:10).

- **Promotes Harmful Narratives**: Conversion therapy promotes harmful narratives that imply that being true to one's identity is inherently wrong or sinful. This teaching contradicts the Gospel's affirmation of every person's inherent worth and dignity. By suggesting that individuals must conform to certain norms to be acceptable, conversion therapy misrepresents the inclusive and affirming nature of the Gospel message (Galatians 5:1, Colossians 3:12-14).

- **Imposes External Standards**: The practices of conversion therapy impose external standards and expectations on individuals, rather than fostering internal transformation through God's love. This approach is contrary to the Gospel's teaching that genuine transformation comes from an authentic relationship with God, not from external pressures or attempts to conform to imposed norms (Matthew 11:28-30, John 15:9-17).

Aligning with the Gospel in Pastoral Care

- **Affirming Unconditional Acceptance**: True pastoral care should reflect the unconditional acceptance and love that the Gospel proclaims. This means supporting individuals in their authentic identities and offering care that is rooted in the recognition of their inherent worth and dignity (1 Peter 4:8, Hebrews 13:1-2).

- **Rejecting Harmful Teachings**: Pastoral care should reject teachings and practices that promote harm or conflict with the Gospel message. Instead, it should provide support that aligns with the transformative power of God's love and grace, fostering an environment where individuals can grow spiritually in a healthy and supportive manner (James 1:27, Matthew 5:14-16).

- **Encouraging Genuine Transformation**: Pastoral care should encourage genuine transformation that stems from a deep and authentic relationship with God. This involves guiding individuals to experience and respond to God's love and grace in ways that reflect the true message of the Gospel, rather than imposing external changes or standards (2 Timothy 1:7, Philippians 1:6).

Conclusion

Conversion therapy provides false teaching contrary to the Gospel by distorting the message of unconditional love, grace, and acceptance central to Christianity. The Gospel affirms the inherent worth of every individual and teaches that genuine transformation comes through a response to God's love and grace, not through coercive or external means. Conversion therapy's harmful practices and narratives undermine these principles, misrepresenting the inclusive and affirming nature of the Gospel. True pastoral care should align with the Gospel by offering unconditional acceptance, rejecting harmful teachings, and encouraging transformation through authentic relationship with God. By doing so, the Church can better reflect the true message of the Gospel and support individuals in their spiritual journey.

43

Conversion therapy sows division within the Church community by creating significant rifts between different groups within the body of Christ. This practice not only contradicts the core teachings of love, unity, and acceptance that should characterize Christian fellowship but also fosters conflict, mistrust, and exclusion among believers. The resulting divisions can weaken the Church's witness and hinder its mission to reflect God's love and unity to the world.

The Biblical Call for Unity and Love

- **Unity in the Body of Christ**: The New Testament consistently calls for unity within the Church. Believers are encouraged to live in harmony, support one another, and work together as one body in Christ. This unity is a reflection of God's love and is essential for the effective witness of the Church to the world (1 Corinthians 1:10, Ephesians 4:3).

- **Love and Acceptance**: Jesus commanded His followers to love one another as He loved them, emphasizing that love is the defining characteristic of Christian community. This love involves acceptance, understanding, and support for one another, regardless of personal differences (John 13:34-35, Romans 13:8-10).

- **Welcoming the Marginalized**: The Gospel teaches that all are welcome in God's family, and the Church should reflect this inclusivity. The message of Christ breaks down barriers and unites people across different backgrounds and identities (Galatians 3:28, Ephesians 2:14).

The Wrongness of Conversion Therapy in Relation to Church Unity

- **Creating Exclusion and Alienation**: Conversion therapy promotes the idea that certain identities or orientations are inherently wrong, leading to the exclusion and alienation of those who do not conform to specific norms. This approach creates a divide between those who are perceived as acceptable and those who are deemed needing correction, undermining the unity and inclusivity that should define the Church community (James 2:1-4, 1 John 4:20).

- **Fostering Conflict and Mistrust**: The presence of conversion therapy within a church community can foster conflict and mistrust among members. It pits those who support the practice against those who oppose it, creating internal strife and division. This conflict distracts from the Church's mission and damages its ability to function as a united body (1 Corinthians 12:25-26, Philippians 2:2).

- **Dividing Families and Friendships**: Conversion therapy can also create division within families and friendships, as individuals who undergo such therapy or support it may be at odds with loved ones who see it as harmful or contrary to their beliefs. This division can strain relationships and lead to long-lasting rifts, impacting the broader Church community (Ephesians 6:1-4, Colossians 3:13).

Promoting Unity and Healing in Pastoral Care

- **Embracing Inclusivity and Respect**: Pastoral care should reflect the inclusivity and respect that are central to the Gospel message. This involves welcoming and supporting all individuals, regardless of their identities or orientations, and working to create a community where everyone feels valued and accepted (Romans 15:7, 1 Peter 4:8).

- **Encouraging Open Dialogue**: Fostering unity involves encouraging open and respectful dialogue about differences within the Church community. This approach helps to address conflicts and misunderstandings in a way that promotes healing and reconciliation rather than division (Proverbs 15:1, Matthew 18:15-17).

- **Focusing on Shared Mission and Purpose**: The Church should focus on its shared mission and purpose, emphasizing common goals and values that unite its members. By prioritizing the Gospel's message of love and service, the Church can overcome divisions and work together to fulfill its mission (Philippians 1:27, Colossians 3:14-15).

Conclusion

Conversion therapy sows division within the Church community by promoting exclusion, fostering conflict, and creating rifts among believers. This practice undermines the unity and inclusivity that are central to the Gospel message, which calls for love, acceptance, and harmony among all members of the body of Christ. True pastoral care should focus on embracing inclusivity, encouraging open dialogue, and prioritizing the shared mission of the Church to promote unity and healing. By rejecting conversion therapy and working towards a more unified and supportive community, the Church can better reflect God's love and fulfill its calling to be a place of acceptance and reconciliation.

44

Conversion therapy often ignores the context and historical background of Scripture, leading to a misapplication of biblical texts and principles. Understanding the historical and cultural context of the Bible is crucial for interpreting its teachings accurately and applying them appropriately to contemporary issues. The misuse of Scripture in support of conversion therapy reflects a lack of attention to the broader context in which biblical passages were written, resulting in interpretations that can be harmful and contrary to the message of love and grace central to Christianity.

The Importance of Context and Historical Background in Biblical Interpretation

- **Historical and Cultural Context**: The Bible was written in specific historical and cultural contexts that influenced its messages and teachings. Understanding these contexts is essential for interpreting Scripture accurately and discerning how its principles apply to modern issues. Ignoring this context can lead to misinterpretations that do not align with the original intent of the biblical authors (Acts 17:11, 2 Timothy 2:15).

- **Literary and Theological Context**: Biblical passages must be understood within their literary and theological contexts. This means considering the genre, purpose, and message of the text, as well as how it fits within the broader narrative of Scripture. Misapplying verses without this context can distort their meaning and lead to teachings that diverge from the core message of the Gospel (1 Corinthians 2:13, Hebrews 4:12).

- **Progressive Revelation**: The Bible reveals God's will progressively, culminating in the life and teachings of Jesus Christ. Understanding this progressive revelation helps in interpreting how Old Testament laws and practices relate to the New Testament message of grace and love. Misunderstanding this progression can lead to applying outdated or culturally specific practices to contemporary issues (Matthew 5:17, Galatians 3:24-25).

The Wrongness of Conversion Therapy in Relation to Biblical Context

- **Misinterpreting Biblical Texts**: Conversion therapy often relies on selective or out-of-context biblical texts to justify its practices. For example, passages related to sexual behavior are sometimes interpreted in ways that do not take into account the historical and cultural context of ancient Israel or the broader message of the New Testament. This selective interpretation can lead to teachings that are not faithful to the original intent of Scripture (2 Peter 3:16, Acts 15:19-20).

- **Ignoring the Message of Love and Grace**: By focusing narrowly on certain texts, conversion therapy ignores the overarching message of love, grace, and acceptance that characterizes the Gospel. Jesus' ministry emphasized compassion and inclusion, and the New Testament teaches that God's grace is available to all people. Misusing Scripture to support conversion therapy contradicts this central message and fails to account for the full scope of biblical teaching (John 3:17, Romans 5:8).

- **Cultural and Historical Disconnect**: Conversion therapy often disregards the cultural and historical differences between ancient practices and contemporary issues related to sexual orientation and gender identity. Applying ancient laws or cultural norms to modern contexts without considering their original purpose and relevance can lead to harmful and inappropriate practices. This approach fails to recognize the differences between the contexts and results in teachings that are out of step with current understanding and compassion (1 Corinthians 9:22, Colossians 3:16).

Aligning Pastoral Care with Contextual Understanding

- **Educating on Biblical Context**: Pastoral care should involve educating individuals about the historical and cultural context of biblical texts. This helps believers understand Scripture more accurately and apply its teachings in a way that aligns with the overall message of love and grace (Proverbs 4:7, Colossians 1:9).

- **Emphasizing the Gospel Message**: Pastoral care should prioritize the core message of the Gospel, which centers on God's love and grace rather than on specific legalistic interpretations. This approach encourages a more holistic understanding of Scripture that reflects the inclusive and compassionate nature of Jesus' teachings (Ephesians 2:8-9, 1 John 4:7).

- **Promoting Compassionate Application**: Applying biblical principles with compassion and respect for contemporary issues involves considering the broader implications of Scripture's teachings. Pastoral care should seek to address modern concerns in ways that honor the historical context of the Bible while reflecting its core messages of love and acceptance (Matthew 7:12, Galatians 5:22-23).

Conclusion

Conversion therapy ignores the context and historical background of Scripture by misinterpreting biblical texts and failing to consider the broader message of the Bible. This approach distorts the teachings of Scripture and contradicts the core principles of love, grace, and acceptance central to the Gospel. True biblical interpretation requires understanding the historical, cultural, and literary contexts of biblical passages and applying them in ways that align with the overall message of Christianity. By rejecting conversion therapy and focusing on compassionate and contextually informed pastoral care, the Church can better reflect the inclusive and grace-filled message of the Gospel.

45

Conversion therapy neglects the principle that "mercy triumphs over judgment," a core biblical teaching that emphasizes God's preference for compassion and forgiveness over condemnation. This principle is fundamental to the Christian understanding of God's relationship with humanity and should guide all pastoral care and theological practice. Conversion therapy, with its focus on changing individuals through coercive means and its often judgmental approach, stands in stark contrast to this principle, which underscores the importance of extending mercy, understanding, and grace to others.

Biblical Foundation of Mercy Over Judgment

- **Mercy as Central to God's Nature**: The Bible repeatedly emphasizes that God's nature is characterized by mercy and compassion rather than judgment and condemnation. God's mercy is extended to all people, reflecting His desire to forgive and restore rather than punish (Micah 7:18, Psalm 103:8).

- **Jesus' Teachings on Mercy**: Jesus' ministry was marked by acts of mercy and forgiveness. He consistently challenged the prevailing judgmental attitudes of His time, advocating for love, acceptance, and the transformation of the heart rather than external compliance (Matthew 9:13, Luke 6:36).

- **Mercy in the New Testament**: The New Testament reinforces the principle that mercy should triumph over judgment. James 2:13 states, "Mercy triumphs over judgment," highlighting that God's mercy is more powerful and desirable than strict adherence to judgmental standards. This principle encourages believers to reflect God's mercy in their interactions with others (1 Peter 1:3, Ephesians 2:4-5).

The Wrongness of Conversion Therapy in Relation to Mercy Over Judgment

- **Imposing Judgment Rather Than Offering Mercy**: Conversion therapy often operates from a judgmental perspective, aiming to correct what it perceives as moral failings or deviations from certain norms. This approach focuses on imposing change and can lead to significant harm, neglecting the biblical principle that mercy should guide our interactions with others. Instead of extending compassion and understanding, conversion therapy promotes an agenda of correction and condemnation (Matthew 7:1-2, Luke 18:9-14).

- **Fostering Shame and Fear**: Conversion therapy frequently uses shame and fear as tools to coerce individuals into conforming to specific norms. This approach is antithetical to the message of mercy, which seeks to uplift and support individuals rather than punish or isolate them. The focus on changing behavior through fear and shame contradicts the biblical call to approach others with compassion and grace (Romans 8:1, 1 John 4:18).

- **Overlooking the Transformative Power of Mercy**: The principle that mercy triumphs over judgment emphasizes the transformative power of compassion and forgiveness. Conversion therapy's focus on external change through coercion disregards the potential for true transformation that comes from experiencing and responding to God's mercy. Genuine change is most effectively nurtured through a relationship with God that is grounded in love and grace, rather than through judgmental or punitive measures (2 Corinthians 5:17, Titus 3:5).

Aligning Pastoral Care with the Principle of Mercy

- **Extending Compassion and Understanding**: Pastoral care should embody the principle of mercy by extending compassion and understanding to all individuals. This involves supporting people in their authentic selves and offering care that reflects the love and grace of God, rather than focusing on judgment or correction (Colossians 3:12-13, Galatians 6:1-2).

- **Promoting Genuine Transformation through Love**: True transformation is fostered through experiences of God's love and grace, which are central to the principle of mercy. Pastoral care should emphasize the nurturing power of God's mercy, helping individuals grow spiritually and personally through supportive and loving relationships (Ephesians 4:15, 1 Thessalonians 5:11).

- **Rejecting Judgmental Practices**: Pastoral care should reject practices that are judgmental or coercive. Instead, it should focus on creating an environment where individuals feel valued and accepted, reflecting the mercy that triumphs over judgment. This approach aligns with the teachings of Jesus and the overall message of the Gospel (Matthew 11:28-30, James 2:13).

Conclusion

Conversion therapy neglects the principle that "mercy triumphs over judgment," a fundamental biblical teaching that underscores the importance of compassion and grace over condemnation. By focusing on coercion and judgment, conversion therapy contradicts the core message of the Gospel, which calls for extending mercy and understanding to others. True pastoral care should align with this principle by promoting compassion, supporting genuine transformation through love, and rejecting judgmental practices. Embracing the principle of mercy allows the Church to better reflect the inclusive and grace-filled message of Jesus and to foster a supportive and loving community.

46

Conversion therapy distracts from the Church's mission of love and service by shifting focus from the core Christian call to love others unconditionally and serve those in need, to a controversial and divisive practice that can undermine the Church's credibility and effectiveness in fulfilling its mission. The focus on changing individuals through coercive and harmful means diverts attention and resources away from the Church's primary purpose of embodying Christ's love and extending compassionate service to all.

The Church's Mission of Love and Service

- **Love as the Central Commandment**: Jesus emphasized love as the greatest commandment, directing His followers to love God with all their hearts and to love their neighbors as themselves (Matthew 22:37-40). This command encompasses all aspects of Christian life and should be the guiding principle for the Church's mission and activities.

- **Service to Others**: The New Testament teaches that Christians are called to serve others selflessly, reflecting Christ's example of humble service. Jesus modeled this service through His life and ministry, and He instructed His followers to do likewise, prioritizing acts of compassion, justice, and support for those in need (Mark 10:45, John 13:12-17).

- **Witness to the World**: The Church is called to be a witness to the world by demonstrating the transformative power of God's love. This witness involves living out the principles of love, grace, and service in ways that draw others to Christ and reflect His character (Matthew 5:14-16, John 13:35).

The Wrongness of Conversion Therapy in Relation to the Church's Mission

- **Diverting Focus from Core Mission**: Conversion therapy can divert the Church's focus away from its core mission of love and service.

By prioritizing the controversial and harmful practice of trying to change individuals' sexual orientation or gender identity, the Church risks neglecting its primary call to love and serve others unconditionally. This misalignment can lead to a diminished ability to fulfill its mission effectively (1 John 4:7, Galatians 5:13).

- **Creating Division and Conflict**: The promotion of conversion therapy can create division and conflict within the Church and the broader community. This divisive issue can distract from the Church's efforts to build unity and work together in service of the Gospel. Such conflict can weaken the Church's witness and hinder its ability to engage in meaningful and collaborative acts of service (1 Corinthians 1:10, Philippians 2:1-2).

- **Damaging the Church's Witness**: Engaging in conversion therapy can damage the Church's witness to the world by projecting an image of intolerance and judgment rather than love and acceptance. This negative perception can undermine the Church's credibility and effectiveness in reaching out to those in need and sharing the message of Christ's love (Matthew 28:19-20, 2 Corinthians 5:20).

Aligning Church Practices with the Mission of Love and Service

- **Focusing on Compassionate Care**: The Church should prioritize compassionate care and support for all individuals, reflecting the love of Christ in its practices and interactions. This includes providing pastoral care that is inclusive, affirming, and aligned with the principles of mercy and understanding (Romans 15:1-2, 1 Peter 4:8).

- **Promoting Unity and Collaboration**: The Church should work to foster unity and collaboration within its community, emphasizing shared values and goals related to service and outreach. By focusing on common missions and working together, the Church can more effectively fulfill its role in the world (Ephesians 4:3, 1 Corinthians 12:4-6).

- **Engaging in Meaningful Service**: The Church should engage in meaningful acts of service that address real needs and challenges in the community. This involves focusing on issues such as poverty, injustice, and support for marginalized groups, rather than becoming entangled in divisive and harmful practices (Micah 6:8, James 1:27).

Conclusion

Conversion therapy distracts from the Church's mission of love and service by focusing on a controversial and harmful practice that diverts attention and resources away from the core call to love others and serve those in need. This misalignment can weaken the Church's witness, create division, and undermine its effectiveness in fulfilling its mission. To remain true to its calling, the Church should prioritize compassionate care, promote unity, and engage in meaningful service that reflects the love of Christ and addresses the needs of the community. By aligning its practices with the mission of love and service, the Church can better fulfill its role in embodying the Gospel and making a positive impact in the world.

47

Conversion therapy violates the fundamental human rights of individuals by infringing upon their personal dignity, autonomy, and freedom from harm. These rights are universally recognized as essential to human dignity and are protected under various international human rights frameworks. Conversion therapy's coercive and harmful methods undermine these rights, often leading to significant psychological, emotional, and social damage.

Fundamental Human Rights at Stake

- **Right to Personal Dignity**: Every individual has the right to be treated with inherent dignity and respect. Conversion therapy, by attempting to alter deeply personal aspects of one's identity, disregards this fundamental right and treats individuals as problems to be fixed rather than as persons worthy of respect and care (Genesis 1:27, Psalm 139:14).

- **Right to Autonomy**: Autonomy is the right of individuals to make their own choices about their lives and bodies. Conversion therapy often disregards this right by coercing individuals into attempting to change their sexual orientation or gender identity, undermining their ability to make personal decisions freely and authentically (Galatians 5:13, 1 Corinthians 6:12).

- **Right to Freedom from Harm**: Individuals have the right to be free from physical and psychological harm. Conversion therapy can inflict significant emotional and psychological damage, leading to anxiety, depression, and even suicidal ideation. The practice of subjecting individuals to such harmful methods violates their right to safety and well-being (Jeremiah 29:11, 3 John 1:2).

The Wrongness of Conversion Therapy in Relation to Human Rights

- **Coercive Methods**: Conversion therapy often employs coercive techniques that pressure individuals into conforming to specific sexual orientations or gender identities. This coercion undermines personal autonomy and violates the principle of informed consent, as individuals may be subjected to practices without their genuine agreement or understanding of potential harms (Ephesians 5:11, Romans 12:2).

- **Psychological and Emotional Harm**: The psychological and emotional harm inflicted by conversion therapy directly contradicts the right to freedom from harm. Many individuals subjected to these practices experience severe mental health issues, including depression, anxiety, and a diminished sense of self-worth. Such outcomes are a clear violation of their human rights and contradict the principles of respect and care that should guide pastoral practices (Matthew 11:28-30, 1 Peter 5:7).

- **Disregard for Individual Identity**: Conversion therapy often involves efforts to change fundamental aspects of an individual's identity, such as their sexual orientation or gender identity. This disregard for a person's inherent identity and experiences undermines their dignity and violates their right to live authentically and be accepted for who they are (1 Corinthians 12:18, Colossians 3:10).

Upholding Human Rights in Pastoral Care

- **Respect for Autonomy and Consent**: Pastoral care should honor the autonomy and consent of individuals by ensuring that all interactions and support are based on mutual respect and genuine agreement. This includes providing care that respects individuals' choices and identity, rather than attempting to coerce or alter their fundamental selves (Romans 14:4, James 1:19).

- **Promoting Mental and Emotional Well-being**: The Church should prioritize the mental and emotional well-being of individuals by offering support that fosters health and wholeness. This involves providing compassionate care that avoids harm and promotes positive outcomes for individuals (Philippians 4:6-7, 1 Thessalonians 5:11).

- **Affirming Individual Identity**: Pastoral care should affirm and support individuals in their authentic identities, recognizing and valuing them as they are. This approach aligns with respecting human dignity and rights, and reflects the inclusive and accepting nature of Christian love (Galatians 3:28, 1 John 4:7).

Conclusion

Conversion therapy violates fundamental human rights by infringing upon personal dignity, autonomy, and the right to freedom from harm. The coercive and harmful nature of this practice contradicts the principles of respect and care central to Christian teaching. To align with human rights and Christian values, pastoral care should prioritize respect for individual autonomy, promote mental and emotional well-being, and affirm the authentic identities of all individuals. By rejecting conversion therapy and embracing practices that honor human dignity and rights, the Church can better fulfill its mission of love and support for all people.

48

Conversion therapy often relies more on human methods than on prayer and divine intervention, which underscores its misalignment with core Christian principles. The focus on human-driven techniques and strategies to alter an individual's sexual orientation or gender identity reflects a departure from spiritual reliance on God and His transformative power. This reliance on human methods rather than divine intervention can undermine the essence of Christian faith and pastoral care.

The Christian Foundation of Prayer and Divine Intervention

- **Prayer as a Means of Seeking God's Will**: In Christianity, prayer is a fundamental practice through which believers seek God's guidance, intervention, and will. Jesus taught His followers to pray, emphasizing the importance of relying on God's power rather than human strength alone (Matthew 6:9-13, Philippians

4:6). Prayer is meant to align individuals with God's will and invite His transformative power into their lives.

- **Divine Intervention in Transformation**: Christian teaching holds that true transformation comes through divine intervention rather than solely human effort. The Holy Spirit plays a crucial role in guiding and changing hearts and lives. This transformation is seen as a work of God, not merely the result of human methods or practices (2 Corinthians 5:17, Galatians 5:22-23).

- **Biblical Examples of Divine Healing and Change**: The Bible provides numerous examples of God's intervention in bringing about healing and change. Jesus performed miracles and offered healing through divine power, demonstrating that true change and healing come from God's work rather than human techniques (John 5:8-9, Luke 8:43-48).

The Wrongness of Conversion Therapy in Relation to Prayer and Divine Intervention

- **Human-Centered Approaches**: Conversion therapy often relies on psychological techniques, behavioral modification, and other human-centered approaches to attempt to change an individual's sexual orientation or gender identity. This focus on human methods can overshadow the role of prayer and divine intervention, which are central to Christian belief and practice (Proverbs 3:5-6, Jeremiah 33:3).

- **Neglecting Spiritual Guidance**: By focusing on human-driven methods, conversion therapy can neglect the importance of seeking God's guidance and intervention through prayer. This approach misses the opportunity to align individuals with God's will and the transformative power of His grace, potentially leading to ineffective or harmful outcomes (James 1:5, 1 Thessalonians 5:17).

- **Potential for Harm Over Healing**: The reliance on human methods in conversion therapy can lead to practices that are harmful rather than healing. Instead of seeking God's intervention and guidance, conversion therapy's techniques can inflict psychological and emotional damage, contrary to the goal of bringing about genuine transformation through divine means (Matthew 7:7-8, 2 Timothy 1:7).

Embracing Prayer and Divine Intervention in Pastoral Care

- **Prioritizing Prayer in Support**: Pastoral care should prioritize prayer as a means of seeking God's guidance, healing, and transformation. This involves praying for individuals and encouraging them to seek God's will and intervention in their lives. Prayer supports a compassionate and spiritually

grounded approach to care
(Philippians 4:6, Colossians 4:2).

- **Encouraging Reliance on Divine Power**: Pastoral care should encourage individuals to rely on divine power rather than solely on human methods. This includes fostering an environment where individuals can experience God's grace and transformation through spiritual practices and support that align with Christian teachings (Ephesians 3:20, Romans 12:2).

- **Integrating Faith with Care**: Effective pastoral care integrates faith with practical support, acknowledging the role of divine intervention in addressing personal struggles. This approach respects the individual's identity and experiences while emphasizing the importance of God's transformative power (Hebrews 11:6, 1 Peter 5:7).

Conclusion

Conversion therapy's reliance on human methods rather than prayer and divine intervention reflects a misalignment with core Christian principles. By focusing on human-driven techniques to alter an individual's sexual orientation or gender identity, conversion therapy neglects the importance of seeking God's guidance and transformative power. True Christian pastoral care should prioritize prayer and divine intervention, aligning with the teachings of Jesus and the work of the Holy Spirit. Embracing these spiritual practices ensures that support and care are grounded in faith, compassion, and the transformative power of God.

49

Conversion therapy fosters self-loathing rather than self-acceptance in God's love, fundamentally contradicting the Christian principles of inherent worth and divine love. By attempting to change an individual's sexual orientation or gender identity through coercive methods, conversion therapy often leads to internalized self-hatred and a diminished sense of self-worth, rather than helping individuals embrace their identity as beloved children of God.

The Christian Principle of Self-Acceptance in God's Love

- **Inherent Worth and Dignity**: Christianity teaches that every person is created in the image of God and possesses inherent worth and dignity. This belief is grounded in the idea that all individuals are valuable and loved by God just as they are. Self-acceptance stems from recognizing and embracing this divine love and inherent worth (Genesis 1:27, Psalm 139:14).

- **God's Unconditional Love**: The New Testament emphasizes that God's love is unconditional and all-encompassing. Jesus' teachings highlight that God loves all people regardless of their circumstances or personal struggles. Embracing this love involves accepting oneself as God accepts them, without conditions or attempts to change fundamental aspects of their identity (John 3:16, Romans 5:8).

- **Call to Love One Another**: Jesus commanded His followers to love others as themselves, which implies a healthy self-acceptance rooted in recognizing one's own worth and the love of God. This self-acceptance enables individuals to extend love and compassion to others, aligning with the core message of Christianity (Matthew 22:39, 1 John 4:7).

The Wrongness of Conversion Therapy in Relation to Self-Acceptance

- **Inducing Self-Loathing**: Conversion therapy often uses shame, fear, and guilt to attempt to alter an individual's sexual orientation or gender identity. These methods can lead to feelings of self-loathing and inadequacy, as individuals are made to feel that their true selves are unacceptable. This internalized self-hatred is in direct contradiction to the Christian message of accepting oneself as loved by God (Romans 8:1, 1 John 4:18).

- **Undermining Self-Worth**: By suggesting that a person's identity is something that needs to be changed, conversion therapy undermines their sense of self-worth and value. It sends the message that who they are is inherently flawed or sinful, rather than recognizing them as created in the image of God and worthy of love (Psalm 139:14, Ephesians 2:10).

- **Contradicting Divine Acceptance**: Conversion therapy conflicts with the principle of divine acceptance, which teaches that God loves and accepts people as they are. This approach promotes the idea that change is necessary for acceptance, disregarding the belief that God's love is unconditional and that each person's identity is a reflection of His creation (Romans 15:7, 1 John 3:1).

Fostering Self-Acceptance through Compassionate Pastoral Care

- **Affirming Identity in God's Love**: Pastoral care should focus on affirming individuals' identities as beloved children of God. This involves helping them understand and embrace their worth and dignity as created in God's image, rather than attempting to change or diminish their true selves (Galatians 3:26-28, 1 Peter 2:9).

- **Promoting Healing and Acceptance**: Instead of fostering self-loathing, pastoral care should promote healing and self-acceptance through the message of God's unconditional love. This includes providing support that helps individuals reconcile their identity with their faith and experience the fullness of God's grace and acceptance (2 Corinthians 1:3-4, Ephesians 3:18-19).

- **Encouraging Authentic Living**: Pastoral care should encourage individuals to live authentically, embracing their true selves as part of their spiritual journey. This approach aligns with the Christian understanding that God created each person uniquely and that living authentically is a way of honoring God's creation (1 Thessalonians 2:12, Colossians 3:10).

Conclusion

Conversion therapy fosters self-loathing rather than self-acceptance in God's love by employing methods that induce shame and guilt about one's identity. This approach contradicts the core Christian principles of inherent worth, unconditional love, and divine acceptance. Effective pastoral care should prioritize affirming individuals' identities as beloved children of God, promoting healing and self-acceptance through the message of God's unconditional love. By embracing this compassionate and affirming approach, the Church can better reflect God's love and support individuals in living authentically and with dignity.

50

Conversion therapy undermines the eternal truths of love, acceptance, and grace found in Christ by distorting and contradicting the fundamental principles of Christian faith. The practice's focus on changing individuals' sexual orientation or gender identity through harmful methods runs counter to the core messages of unconditional love, acceptance, and divine grace that are central to the teachings of Jesus.

Eternal Truths of Love, Acceptance, and Grace in Christ

- **Unconditional Love**: Christianity teaches that God's love is unconditional and boundless. Jesus' life and ministry exemplify a love that extends to all people, regardless of their status or identity. This unconditional love is a cornerstone of the Gospel, demonstrating that every person is valued and cherished by God (John 3:16, Romans 5:8).

- **Acceptance of All**: The message of acceptance is woven throughout the New Testament. Jesus reached out to those who were marginalized, rejected, or considered sinful by societal standards, affirming their worth and embracing them with compassion. His acceptance of individuals regardless of their background highlights the inclusive nature of God's love (Luke 15:1-7, John 4:7-30).

- **Grace as a Transformative Power**: Grace is the unmerited favor of God that brings redemption and transformation. Christian teaching emphasizes that grace is available to all people and is not dependent on human efforts or changes in behavior. It is through grace that individuals experience true transformation, not through coercive practices (Ephesians 2:8-9, 2 Corinthians 12:9).

The Wrongness of Conversion Therapy in Relation to Eternal Truths

- **Contradicting Unconditional Love**: Conversion therapy often operates on the premise that individuals' identities are flawed and need to be corrected. This approach fundamentally contradicts the concept of God's unconditional love, which asserts that every person is loved as they are, without conditions or the need for transformation (1 John 4:7-8, Romans 8:38-39).

- **Rejecting Acceptance**: By attempting to change an individual's sexual orientation or gender identity, conversion therapy rejects the principle of acceptance that Jesus modeled. The practice implies that certain identities are unacceptable or unworthy, thereby undermining the inclusive message of Christ's acceptance and affirming that every person is made in the image of God (Genesis 1:27, Galatians 3:28).

- **Misunderstanding Grace**: Conversion therapy suggests that individuals need to alter fundamental aspects of themselves to be acceptable to God, which undermines the concept of grace. Christian teaching holds that grace is given freely and is not contingent upon personal change. The focus on human efforts to achieve change contradicts the Gospel message that transformation comes through God's grace rather than through human striving or coercion (Titus 3:5, Romans 3:24).

Aligning Pastoral Care with Eternal Truths

- **Embracing Unconditional Love**: Pastoral care should reflect the unconditional love of God by accepting and supporting individuals as they are, rather than attempting to change them. This approach honors the divine love that embraces all people and recognizes their inherent worth (1 John 4:16, Matthew 22:39).

- **Practicing True Acceptance**: Effective pastoral care involves practicing true acceptance, which mirrors Jesus' inclusive approach. This means affirming individuals' identities and supporting them in their spiritual journey without imposing conditions or expectations for change (Romans 15:7, Colossians 3:12-14).

- **Proclaiming Grace**: Pastoral care should emphasize the message of grace, which teaches that God's favor is given freely and is not based on human efforts. By focusing on grace, the Church can provide support that reflects the transformative power of God's love rather than relying on methods that seek to coerce change (Hebrews 4:16, 2 Timothy 1:9).

Conclusion

Conversion therapy undermines the eternal truths of love, acceptance, and grace found in Christ by promoting methods that are contrary to these core Christian principles. It challenges the unconditional nature of God's love, rejects the inclusive acceptance modeled by Jesus, and misunderstands the concept of grace as unmerited favor. To align with the eternal truths of Christianity, pastoral care should reflect God's unconditional love, practice true acceptance, and proclaim the transformative power of grace. By doing so, the Church can better embody the message of Christ and support individuals in their authentic identity as beloved children of God.

www.ingramcontent.com/pod-product-compliance
Lightning Source LLC
Chambersburg PA
CBHW070818250726
48662CB00003B/1007